A PILGRIM'S JOURNEY

A Devotional Journey of Trust and Obedience

REVISED EDITION

MARC TURNAGE

SALUBRIS
RESOURCES

Published by Salubris Resources
1445 N. Boonville Ave.
Springfield, Missouri 65802
www.salubrisresources.com

Cover and interior design by Prodigy Pixel (www.prodigypixel.com)

Unless otherwise specified, all Scripture quotations are
the author's own translation.

ISBN: 978-1-68067-115-5

19 18 17 16 ● 1 2 3 4 5

Printed in the United States of America

CONTENTS

INTRODUCTION

This devotional, *A Pilgrim's Journey*, originally began as a thirty-day devotional for participants on the study tours of the Center for Holy Lands Studies. It still is. But as it came together, we realized this book wasn't simply for those journeying the miles to the land of the Bible; no, we're all on a journey in need of encountering the three-dimensional realities of our faith. The Bible is God's revelation in time and place. His ultimate revelation was Jesus, who entered time and space at a specific moment in history. For this reason, location and history have played a uniquely important role in Judaism and Christianity. The two principal acts of redemption in the Bible—the Exodus from Egypt and Jesus' resurrection—assume God's activity in history at a specific time and in a specific place. This fundamental belief has resulted in Jews and Christians feeling a particular attachment to the land in which God acted, the land of Israel. Over millennia, countless pilgrims have journeyed from around the world to enter the three-dimensional space where God revealed Himself.

Judaism and Christianity have a long history of pilgrimage. In the Old Testament, God commanded, "Three times a year all your males will appear before" Him (Ex. 23:17; 34:23; Deut. 16:16). As Jerusalem became the center of Judaism, both politically and religiously, it became the heart of pilgrimage, as attested by the actions of Jesus and His family and Paul (Luke 2:41; John 5:1; Acts 20:16). Pilgrims,

both Jews and God-fearing Gentiles, streamed from the four corners of the world to worship God in the place where He caused His
name to dwell.

Many of these pilgrims saved their money and prepared for years
to make the journey; it was the moment of a lifetime. Often families and villages traveled together for the festivals in Jerusalem. It
became a community experience and celebration. As they arrived
in Jerusalem, they purified themselves in the ritual immersion
pools that have been excavated all over Jerusalem (Acts 21:26),
approaching the temple mount complex from a series of stairs
coming from the south. As they ascended the mountain of the Lord,
they sang the Psalms of Ascent (Ps. 120–134). It must have been an
incredible moment in their lives.

In more recent times, as pilgrims have sought to enter into the space
of the Bible, to see the locations mentioned by the biblical writers—
Jerusalem, Bethlehem, Capernaum, and Nazareth—they have often
failed to interact properly with the temporal part of God's revelation.
The geography of the Bible played an important role in shaping the
biblical story; in fact, the geography is almost as important a biblical
character as David, Moses, Peter, or Paul. So, too, the Bible is a
product of a specific time in history. In truth, the Bible spans many
eras; the world of Abraham isn't the world of David, nor is the world
of David that of Jesus.

Every Christian community throughout history has framed its understanding of the Bible and spiritual life within the context of its own
culture. This proves challenging for many Christians because the
world of Jesus is not my world or yours. The Bible and the personal-
ities mentioned in it are the products of a a culture that evolved over
time and was shaped by the land in which the people lived. In this
way, the people of the Bible, even Jesus, are like you and me in that

they, too, came from somewhere. Where they grew up affected how they viewed and understood the world. They were no less shaped by the times in which they lived than we are.

Visiting the land of the Bible is only one aspect of understanding God's revelation in time and place. There are four aspects of studying the Bible and visiting Israel: (1) *spatial*—the geography is the stage of the biblical story; (2) *historical*—the Bible reflects the history of the Jewish people and the land of Israel over hundreds of years; (3) *cultural*—the Bible must be read within the context of its contemporary culture; and (4) *spiritual*—the Bible reflects the religious beliefs and outlooks of the ancient writers. Traveling to the land of Israel enables Christians to encounter these four aspects of the Bible in the place where much of it happened. In this way, the land provides the three-dimensional doorway for you to enter into the time and culture of God's revelation in order to hear and see the Bible as its ancient readers would have. This enables God to speak to you in new and fresh ways.

This devotional is for those on a journey—whether a trip to the lands of the Bible or life's journey. Ancient pilgrims prepared themselves before they left their homes. They committed themselves to the journey—the labors of travel, the dangers, the cost of time and money, and the unknown experiences that awaited them along the way. Throughout the journey, even arriving at their destination of the temple in Jerusalem, ancient pilgrims recited the Psalms of Ascent (Ps. 120–134),[1] which is why the first fifteen days of this devotional focus on these psalms.

The journey of the ancient pilgrims took them to a place, to a land, and to a city. Because the Bible is God's revelation in time and place, location matters in our understanding of it. The next seven days of this devotional provide spiritual lessons based on physical settings of the biblical world. The Bible also represents a cultural world much different from our own. In order to properly understand any part of the Bible, including Jesus and His message, we must read it within its cultural context. The next seven days of this devotional provide an example of reading the different phrases of the Lord's Prayer within the context of first-century Judaism, which was an integral part of Jesus' life.

Finally, God's clearest and greatest revelation of Himself is Jesus, who entered time and space at a specific moment in history. The final devotion of this thirty-day journey reflects on the song of the angels to the shepherds announcing the birth of Jesus, the sign that God is with us. As you learn to read the Bible through the lenses of space, time, culture, and spirituality, you'll find its message bridging time and space to transform how you live in the twenty-first century.

For those traveling on a study trip with the Center for Holy Lands Studies, the Center uniquely incorporates these four aspects into your journey. Many tours solely emphasize the spatial aspect, "standing where Jesus stood." It is our belief that by viewing the Bible through these four dimensions, participants will hear the biblical message, especially the message of Jesus, anew and afresh. Our prayer is that your program will be an educational and spiritual encounter with the God of Abraham, Isaac, and Jacob, and that, like the disciples on the road to Emmaus, you will say, "Were not our hearts burning within us while he was talking to us on the road, while he was opening the scriptures to us" (Luke 24:32).

In addition to this pre-trip devotional, your experience will be greatly enhanced if portions of the Bible are fresh in your mind. Therefore, we strongly encourage you to read the following biblical passages prior to your trip:

- Genesis 12–50
- Exodus 1–20
- Joshua 1–10
- Judges
- Samuel/Kings
- Psalm 42 and the Psalms of Ascent (120–134)
- Luke
- Acts 1–10

Our hope is that your trip will transform your study and understanding of the Bible, and you will return home with a renewed commitment "to study the Law of the LORD and to do it" (Ezra 7:10).

The suggested Scripture readings, reflections, questions, and prayers are meant to provide an opportunity for God to speak to you through His Word, providing insight into His plan for you and preparing you for what He wants to do in and through you.

1. Read the daily devotional in *A Pilgrim's Journey*.

2. Read the suggested Scripture readings for the day.

3. Think about the recommended reflections and questions, perhaps recording your responses in a journal.

4. Pray the short prayer as a starting point for your own prayer and response.

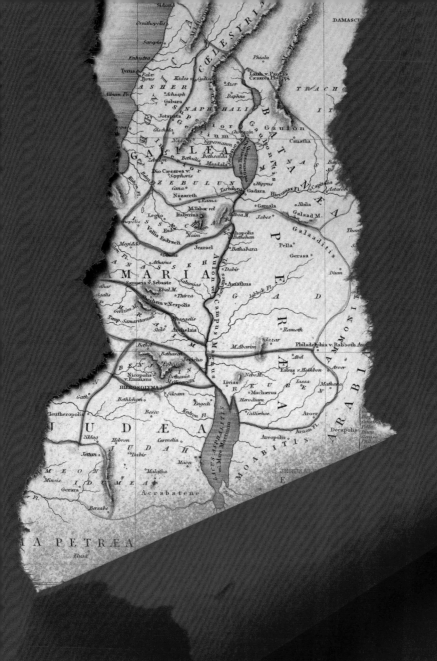

SETTING YOUR HEART ON PILGRIMAGE

Woe is me, that I am an alien in Meshech, that I
must live among the tents of Kedar.

PSALM 120:5

The Psalms of Ascent (Ps. 120–134) eventually became psalms recited by Jewish pilgrims traveling to Jerusalem to appear before the Lord. Psalm 120 provides an appropriate opening to the Psalms of Ascent because the psalmist uses geographic isolation from Jerusalem to describe his feelings of being removed far from Jerusalem and the God of peace while dwelling among people of violence in a world of chaos. With this recognition, the psalmist decides to free himself from his current state and move toward God and Jerusalem.

Meshech most likely refers to a region in the far north of Israel, south of the Black Sea. The inhabitants of the region were a warlike mountain people (Gen. 10:2; Ezek. 32:26). Kedar refers to the nomadic tribes of the Arabian desert far to the southeast of the land of Israel and Jerusalem. Within the ancient Near East, the Kedarenes were regarded as specialists in bowmanship. Riding on their camels, they were feared raiders who attacked villages, murdering and plundering (Isa. 21:13–17; Jer. 49:28–33).

The psalmist doesn't use these two geographic locations to describe his concrete physical location but to articulate his emotional perspective of being at the "end" of his known world, surrounded by warlike peoples and the forces of chaos. While Meshech and Kedar represented the borders of the world of the psalmist, they also embodied locations removed from Jerusalem, the center of the world for Israelites.

The psalmist feels surrounded by chaos and violence and removed from Zion and God. Yet he reminds himself of the past, when in his distress he called to the Lord and the Lord answered him (Ps. 120:1). He feels out-of-lockstep with his world, dwelling among those who hate peace, yet he is for peace (vv. 6–7). At the same time, he feels tainted by the chaos and violence that surround him (vv. 2, 6). In verse 6, he expresses a desire to break free from his surroundings and move toward Jerusalem, the city of peace (Ps. 122), and toward God.

A pilgrimage isn't merely a trip to a parcel of holy ground; rather, it begins with recognizing how far the world around us removes us from the God of peace. With this realization, we begin the process of freeing ourselves from the oppression of this world and moving toward Jerusalem and God—in either a physical or metaphorical sense.

In the ancient world, people living outside of Jerusalem generally only made the pilgrimage to Jerusalem once in their lives. Such a journey wasn't something they approached frivolously. They prepared themselves both before embarking and along the way to appear before the God of Israel.

The writer of Psalm 120 recognized that often the world we live in and the people around us influence us and create a sense of separation from God. We find ourselves in the midst of chaos, feeling like we're at the end of our world. Any pilgrimage begins with a conscious decision to move from where we are to where we cried out to God and He answered us, even from the ends of the earth (Ps. 61:2–3).

SCRIPTURE READINGS:

- Read Psalms 120 and 61.
- Describe a time when you felt distant from God.
- What did you do or should you do to draw closer to God?
- Why do you think the idea of pilgrimage was important in ancient times?
- How do you think a pilgrimage to the land of the Bible will change you?

PRAYER

Lord, when I am troubled, hear my cry and answer me.

When I am caught up in the worries of this life, deliver me.

When I am far from You, draw me close.

When I feel there is distance, let me feel Your peaceful embrace.

LOOKING TO GOD

———

I will lift my eyes to the mountains, from where my help comes;
my help comes from the LORD, the creator of heaven and earth.

PSALM 121:1–2

I n Psalm 121, the psalmist finds himself in the midst of a world filled with dangers (vv. 3–8), so he looks expectantly and with confidence to the God of Israel, the Maker of heaven and earth who dwells on the mountains of Israel. In the Old Testament, the phrase "lift the eyes toward" carries a sense of desire, to look toward something with longing (Gen. 39:7; Ezek. 18:6, 12; 23:27; Jer. 3:2). In the context of Psalm 121, the psalmist looks with longing toward the place where the Lord is present, helping those who look to Him—the mountains of Zion (Ps. 133:3).

The psalmist is aware of the dangers that will beset him along his journey, yet from the outset he confidently turns his eyes toward the Lord as his companion and the source of his protection. Unlike in Psalm 120, where the psalmist feels overwhelmed by the chaos of his circumstances, in Psalm 121, he realizes he can look for help from the God who created everything. The psalmist confesses his confidence that the Lord will help him and protect him. The nearness of the Lord is made particularly poignant by his use of the participle "creator of (literally, the One making) heaven and earth." By using this language, the psalmist voices his deep conviction that the God of Israel is continually attentive to His world and continues to protect it and keep it alive.

The psalmist doesn't ignore the dangers of life, yet he analyzes those dangers through the reality of a God who is attentive to His creation and stands ready to help in moments of distress. The Bible consistently describes God as One who watches over His people, guarding them (Gen. 28:15, 20; Num. 6:24; Josh. 24:17). The psalmist intentionally contrasts the Lord against the motif of resting and sleeping deities within the ancient Near Eastern world (1 Kings 18:27). Unlike the deities of other peoples and human beings themselves, the God of Israel does "not slumber" or waver in His vigilance over His people (Ps. 121:3).

In Psalm 120, the psalmist uses Meshech and Kedar, the edges of his world, to create a horizontal worldview. In Psalm 121, he establishes a vertical worldview by using "heaven and earth," "sun and moon." He has moved from an overwhelming sense of chaos to a point of confident trust in the God of Israel, the one enthroned on the mountains of Zion, as his protector. The psalmist is traveling to Jerusalem, the city that will shelter him (Ps. 122) from the dangerous, chaotic, and warlike world in which he finds himself. Psalm 121 acts as a "blessing for the journey" for a person traveling to Jerusalem.

Our world often overwhelms us with feelings of despair. As we look at the chaos around us, we might feel like we're at the end of the earth; yet when we set our hearts on pilgrimage, to draw near to God, a change takes place. The dangers of the journey don't diminish, but we gain an incredible sense that God journeys with us to protect and watch over us. We look to Him with confidence and trust, knowing He will bring us safely to Jerusalem, the city of peace that will shelter us from the chaos of the world. The challenge, however, is that circumstances and the world around us often clamor with doubts: "Surely if there is a God, He can't be involved and interested in us; just look at the world around us!" But the God of the Bible is attentive to His world and to the cry of His people. He neither slumbers nor sleeps in His watchful care over our journey.

SCRIPTURE READINGS:

- Read Psalms 121 and 73.
- What are your first reactions to feelings of danger, chaos, or being overwhelmed? *Anxiousness*
- Why do you think you respond this way? *– Fear; lack of trust/faith*
- Describe a time when God helped you. *– so many times – Healed me, provided for me*
- How do you need God's help today? *Good biopsy results – He has given me His peace – tho I have had to battle some fear when a thought comes in*

PRAYER

Lord, help me to look to You when I am overwhelmed.

Lead me, comfort me, and keep me safe.

Keep me from doing something wrong and hurting others when I am distressed.

Be with me as I go out and as I come back home.

ARRIVING IN THE GATES OF THE LORD

---

*I was glad when they said to me, "Let us go to the house of the
Lord!" Our feet are standing in your gates, O Jerusalem.*

PSALM 122:1-2

I f you read Psalms 120–122 as a unit, you detect a movement
from the margins of the world to Jerusalem as the world's center.
It's the movement of a pilgrim journeying from far away to the
house of the Lord in Jerusalem. At the outset and along the journey (Ps. 120–121), the pilgrim feels isolated, surrounded by violence
and chaos, exposed to the dangers of the journey, and yearning to
arrive in Jerusalem (Ps. 122), where one finds the safety and protection of the house of the Lord. Within Jerusalem's gates, pilgrims find
security, justice, and peace.

The mention of the house of the Lord in verses 1 and 9 emphasizes
that the psalmist isn't speaking metaphorically but referring to
the physical Jerusalem where the house of the Lord stood. While
the temple stood in Jerusalem, the city functioned as the political
(122:5) and spiritual (vv. 1, 9) epicenter of the Jewish people. There,
God caused His name to dwell and established the eternal throne
of the house of David. Imagine the joy and elation the pilgrims felt

as they completed their long journey and arrived in Jerusalem. They had made it; God had brought them safely from a world of chaos and violence to the city of peace. Yet, in the midst of speaking about a physical arrival to the city of Jerusalem, the psalmist betrays an essential assumption of biblical spirituality—he rejoices with the throngs of other pilgrims: "Let us go to the house of the LORD."

Pilgrimage wasn't something a person did alone or in isolation. The pilgrim may have traveled some of the way to Jerusalem alone but would complete most of the journey in the company of other pilgrims. Once they arrived in Jerusalem, they found themselves with other pilgrims who shared the common goal of ascending the mountain of the house of the Lord. Worshipping the Lord in Jerusalem wasn't done in isolation; it occurred in the midst of the community of faith: "To it the tribes go up, the tribes of the LORD . . . to give thanks to the name of the LORD" (v. 4).

We frequently express our spirituality in individualized ways that focus on God and me. Such individualism was foreign to the biblical mind. Worship of God took place with joy in the community of faith. Sin was a problem, in part, because of the damage it brought to the community through broken relations. The journey of the psalmist that began in isolation amid chaos culminated in security in the city of peace before the house of the Lord.

In verses 3–5, the psalmist speaks of Jerusalem's past, historically, politically, and spiritually. One of the key elements of biblical faith is remembering God's actions in the past. The God of the Bible acts in the past, in the present, and in the future. By reflecting on what has happened in the past, in this case Jerusalem's past, it helps us trust God for the present and the future.

In Psalm 120:1, the psalmist recalls a time in his past when he cried to the Lord, and God answered him. In Psalm 122, he reflects on

God's establishment of Jerusalem as the spiritual and political center of the world. There, God dwelt in His house. In Jerusalem, He established the "throne of the house of David" to render justice and mercy. The psalmist mentions Jerusalem's gates and its walls "bound firmly together," but the security and peace of Jerusalem go beyond its gates and walls. It is the dwelling place of the Lord and the throne of the house of David, which He established.

Psalm 120 concludes with a request for the continued peace of Jerusalem, that it will be the center of all who seek peace (Ps. 120:7). The irony, of course, is that rarely in its history has Jerusalem known peace; yet we are enjoined to "pray for the peace of Jerusalem . . . for the sake of my relatives and friends" (Ps. 122:6). In many ways, Jerusalem acts as a microcosm of our world. While it's a city that yearns for peace, historically as well as presently it has been torn apart by social, political, economic, and religious strife. Praying for the peace of Jerusalem is a request for our world, too, as those same forces seek to tear our world apart. It's no wonder that Jesus said to His disciples: "Blessed are the peacemakers, for they will be called children of God" (Matt. 5:9, NIV).

SCRIPTURE READINGS:

- Read Psalm 122 and Matthew 5:21–26.
- Who has helped you the most in your spiritual journey?
- In what ways have they encouraged, corrected, taught, and inspired you?
- Who are the people in your life that you can encourage today?
- Are there any relationships that need the peace of God, where you can be a "peacemaker"?

PRAYER

Lord, thank You for those who have blessed my life.

Thank You for the grace shown to me through others.

I pray for peace in Jerusalem and in our world.

May Your Spirit help me to bring peace in my relationships today.

Z E B
Tanae
Nazareth

Mispah
Itabyrium
rio
S A
Endor
Nain
is Esdraeli

Gilead

tharus
S S E
R E
ebaste Salomons
Ebal M.
Thirza
em v. Neapolis

Phasaelis
A
Shilo Archelao

M

Bethaven
Ephraim
Bethania
Mi
A
Siloam

GOD, OUR KING

As the eyes of servants look to the hand of their master, as the eyes of a maid to the hand of her mistress, so our eyes look to the LORD our God, until He has mercy upon us.

PSALM 123:2

Psalm 123 contains two poignant images: God as King (v. 1) and God as Master (v. 2). These are common themes throughout the Bible. As in Psalm 121, the psalmist lifts up his eyes to the Lord. Again, the use of this phrase "lift up the eyes" assumes desire and expectancy. The psalmist directs his plea specifically to God, whom he describes in royal language as "enthroned in the heavens." For him, God is King over the entire universe.

God alone can answer the cry of His subjects; there is no one else. The psalmist's acknowledgement of God as King not only identifies God as the One who can answer his petition; it also calls upon God's responsibility to hear the cry of His subject. If the cries of the subjects fall on deaf ears, the king stands impotent. The psalmist acknowledges God's kingship and at the same time calls upon the honor of the King as the One who hears the entreaties of His subjects.

The psalmist uses poignant language to describe the state of the people before God as servants waiting for their master to respond to them. The word *maid* actually refers to the lowest of the household slaves, so the psalmist doesn't envision the people as "body" servants but as slaves of the lowest position. This image is dynamic because lowly slaves could receive punishment at the hands of their masters or mistresses. So the image creates a tension as the people wait upon God to see whether His hand will bring punishment or blessing, contempt or restoration. As slaves are completely dependent upon their masters, so God's people remain absolutely dependent upon Him. Yet, as a master bears the responsibility for his slaves, so God's name is at stake in the care He shows to His people. If His people are defeated, He is defeated.

Against these images of the king and the master, the psalmist creates a tension of the responsibilities between God and His people. The people stand completely dependent upon God as the source of all; yet He, being their Master, bears the responsibility for their care. Their defeat marks His defeat. On this basis of dependency and divine responsibility, the psalmist makes his request for mercy (123:3–4).

This tension brings into focus what seem like two diametrically opposed ideas: submission and freedom. Acknowledging God as King and Master requires our submission to Him. His commands should dictate everything we say and do; we are utterly dependent upon Him for everything. He is God, and we are not. As King, He makes the rules and we obey. Yet, within the relationship of a king to his subjects or a master to his slaves lies a freedom—freedom from anxiety and distress. We lift up our eyes to our provider, the source of our entire existence, who bears the responsibility for us. If we submit to Him and are defeated, He fails; His honor is lost. Biblical authors frequently petitioned God based upon His responsibility to His people, calling upon Him to honor His name, which was on display in His people.

In our world, submission and freedom seem like polar opposites. Freedom for us implies the ability to do whatever we want, to control our lives and choices. According to the Bible, such egocentric thinking is *not* freedom but the very essence of sin. God freed the children of Israel from Egyptian bondage so they could serve Him. Through serving Him, they found freedom because He bore the responsibility to care for them.

This confidence led the psalmist to lift his eyes up to the King of the universe, who stands ready to answer and protect His people. How would we live differently if we realized that God's name is at stake in us and that our daily responsibility is to submit to Him? How would we live if we really trusted Him to take care of us?

SCRIPTURE READINGS:

- Read Psalm 123 and 1 Peter 2:9–17. *Authority-Decision-maker*
- When you think of God as King, what images come to your mind?
- When you think of God as Master, what thoughts come to mind? *we are to please Him*
- How does serving God bring freedom?
- How can you honor God as King today?
- How can you use your freedom to honor God as Master today?

Because the weight is on His shoulders - not ours
Respect Him Be loyal; Do what He asks

PRAYER

I praise You, Lord, for You are King.

I serve You, Lord, for You are my Master.

Thank You for the freedom to serve You.

Help me act in ways that bring honor to Your Name.

THE GOD WHO DELIVERS

If it had not been the LORD who was on our side—let Israel now say . . .

PSALM 124:1

P salm 122 brought the pilgrim through the dangers of the journey into the safety of Jerusalem, the city of peace. Psalm 124 brings to a conclusion the arc of tension begun in Psalm 120 when the psalmist cried out to the Lord to be rescued. In Psalm 124, the psalmist presents his crisis in retrospective (vv. 1–5) and turns his words into a song of thanksgiving to the Lord who delivered him. His call for Israel to remember that the Lord is on their side (v. 1) harkens back to Psalm 121, where God is described as the guardian of Israel. This guardian brings the traveler safely into the gates of Jerusalem (Ps. 122); the psalmist experiences God's care and protection.

In the first five verses of Psalm 124, the psalmist remembers God's action in history. Throughout the Bible the writers call upon Israel to remember God's actions: He delivers His people and acts in their history. Unlike the deities of the ancient Near East, the God of Israel "neither slumbers nor sleeps" (Ps. 121:4) in His watchful care for His people. The psalmist uses graphic images to describe the precarious nature of the people's position. Their enemies "would have swallowed us up alive," "the flood would have swept us away," "the torrent would have gone over us" (Ps. 124:3–5). Their circumstances produced a serious existential crisis. The psalmist expresses fear and distress, which reaches a crescendo in the unstoppable, rushing flood waters that unleash their destructive power. Yet in the midst of their helplessness, the God of Israel saved them.

Upon remembering the fear and distress of his situation and God's deliverance, the psalmist responds immediately with thanksgiving. The God of Israel doesn't leave His people to be destroyed. Even if they find themselves pressed on every side, they escape like prey freed from a trap because the Lord is on their side. This leads the psalmist to say, "Our help is in the name of the LORD, who made heaven and earth" (Ps. 121:2). In the Bible, God's name represents His essence. His name is at stake in His people. He shows His divinity and power by rescuing them from death, by acting in time and space.

Crisis has the tendency to breed helplessness and hopelessness. As we feel ourselves swept away in chaos, it seems like circumstances rush over us like a raging torrent. In such moments, it's possible to lose perspective, to lose hope. But if we serve the Lord, the Maker of heaven and earth, then His name is at stake in us. The God of the Bible delights in showing His power by rescuing people from the snares of life, from the jaws of death. In those circumstances, He demonstrates His glory in the world. At times, He even places us in those circumstances to show forth His power and glory.

We tend to have short memories. That's why the act of remembering is so important. By reminding himself and Israel of what God did in the past, the psalmist casts their vision to the future when more enemies will surely arise and more circumstances will threaten to overwhelm them. By remembering God's past deliverance, the psalmist takes a moment for thanksgiving—"Blessed be the LORD" (Ps. 124:6)—which he concludes with a statement of trust in the name of the Lord. This statement of trust is not for the past or the present, but for the future. If God has acted to save us in the past, we can be assured He will do so in the future.

Do we take time to remember? Even though we have come through the floodwaters, when we look back do we only remember the hurts and the difficulties, or do we see God standing at our side and keeping us from being crushed? Does our memory bring forth thanksgiving for the past and confidence for the future?

SCRIPTURE READINGS:

- Read Psalm 124 and Hebrews 12:1–11.
- Describe a time when God used difficulty or hardship to teach you a lesson. What lesson(s) did you learn?
- Make a short list of other difficulties and how God has seen you through them.
- How did you have the opportunity to honor God in each of those circumstances?

PRAYER

Thank You, Lord, for walking with me through times of difficulty.

You have faithfully been my helper and deliverer.

Help me remember the lessons you have taught me, and help me to have confidence in Your provisions.

May I honor Your name throughout the day.

VULNERABLE OBEDIENCE

As the mountains surround Jerusalem, so the LORD surrounds
His people, from this time on and forevermore.

PSALM 125:2

Jerusalem originally developed on the lower spur of what is known as the eastern hill, which is surrounded by higher hills. It was located near a spring known as the Gihon. Because the spring emerged from the ground at the base of the lower part of the eastern hill and flowed into the Kidron Valley, the city built up around the spring. In order to control the water of the spring, Jerusalem gave up elevation, which compromised it strategically. When David conquered Jerusalem, his capital remained on the lower part of the eastern hill. His son Solomon extended the city to the north, where he built his palaces and the temple; yet to the east, south, and west, Jerusalem remained surrounded by higher hills than it, separated from these by the Kidron and Hinnom Valleys. The Assyrian forces of Sennacherib, king of Assyria, exploited this strategic disadvantage when Rabshakeh stood on the Mount of Olives east of Jerusalem and shouted down on the city and its inhabitants dwelling on the eastern hill (2 Kings 18:9–19:37).

Often when people read this psalm, they assume the mountains surrounding Jerusalem provide the image of insulation and security.

In light of the physical setting of Jerusalem, the image means just the opposite—strategic vulnerability.[2] It's never a good thing to give your enemy the higher ground. Yet, the psalmist used Jerusalem's vulnerable topographical position to describe the way God envelops His people, and this is what brings stability and security. As Jerusalem had to depend upon the Lord for its protection, so the people had to depend upon Him for theirs.

In the Bible, Mount Zion referred to the northern portion of the eastern hill where the king's palaces and administrative district stood. The temple, which was erected at the highest point of that hill, represented God's physical dwelling place on earth. It was seen as a place of unshakeable surety. The maxim that one who trusts in the Lord is secure appears often within the Bible (Prov. 29:25). In this instance, the psalmist used the physical/spiritual geography of Mount Zion, the temple mount, to communicate the image of surety. Within verse 1 lurks a hint to a real threat, but against such a threat stands Mount Zion, which is immovable.

After describing the surety of those who trust in the Lord, the God of Israel, and His protective care for His people, the psalmist requests that God protect the land of the righteous, so they might not be led into doing wrong (Ps. 125:3). The psalmist then requests that God do good to those who are good and bring punishment on those who stray from His paths (vv. 4–5). This may strike the modern reader a bit harshly, yet in the Bible, especially in wisdom literature, the idea exists of two ways: one of life and one of death. The difference between them lies in obedience or disobedience to the commandments of God. Moreover, the psalmist viewed the wicked as having the ability to corrupt the righteous if God didn't protect the righteous.

Do we recognize the corrupting power of wickedness around us? We find ourselves inundated with things that oppose God and His ways. Are we sensitive to how such things can corrupt our lives? The biblical mind wrestled with this tension: how to live in obedience to God in a world filled with wickedness that can corrupt. Psalm 125 suggests, "Those who trust in the LORD" (v. 1) are "those who are good, who are upright in their hearts" (v. 4). In other words, trust isn't an emotion; trust is an action. Trust is obedience to the ways of the Lord. Those who obey His ways are like Mount Zion: they cannot be moved. Does our obedience give witness to our trust in the Lord?

SCRIPTURE READINGS:

- Read Psalm 125 and Proverbs 3:1–12.
- Think of a time when it seemed easier to do something that you knew was wrong rather than what you knew was right.
- How did you decide what to do?
- Why does it seem to make us vulnerable when we obey God?
- Why is it better to trust in God rather than in the ways of the world?

PRAYER

Lord, help me to know what to do when my way seems uncertain.

I trust in You and Your word.

Bless me when I obey and correct me when I do not.

Guard my vulnerability with Your strength.

SOWING WITH TEARS

Restore our fortunes, O L<small>ORD</small>, like the watercourses in the Negev.
May those who sow in tears reap with shouts of joy.

The land of Israel provided the biblical authors, poets, and prophets a rich canvas of images and metaphors to describe Israel's experiences. Through the geography, flora, fauna, climate, and agricultural cycle, biblical authors articulated God's message to His people. Psalm 126 is a psalm rejoicing in the return of the exiles from Babylonian captivity: "When the L<small>ORD</small> restored the fortunes of Zion, we were like those who dreamed" (v. 1, NIV). After the desolation wrought by the Babylonian army on the kingdom of Judah and Jerusalem in 586 BC, those returning from exile felt exuberant anticipation, yet they also felt overwhelmed by the task of rebuilding. That feeling of smallness in the midst of an impossible task led the psalmist to request of God: "Restore our fortunes . . . like the watercourses in the Negev."

The land of Israel has several different deserts, each with its own unique features. The Negev, which is in the south of Israel, is a dry land that receives between three and nine inches of rainfall a year. The top layer of soil in the Negev is a wind-blown dust called loess. When rains fall (rarely more than two centimeters in a day), the loess forms an impermeable crust that causes the excess rain to run into the valleys and streambeds. At first this runoff begins in small rivulets, but these rivulets join together in ever-increasing strength until they form rivers that can reach widths of several hundred yards. During these flash floods, the riverbeds of the Negev become raging torrents that suddenly appear and then disappear. The psalmist used this image of water gathering in small rivulets from distant corners of the Negev and coming together in broad streams and rivers to describe his request that, in a similar manner, God would bring His scattered people back to Israel. In this way, God will restore the fortunes of His people.

It's hard for us to imagine a world without supermarkets. They provide everything we need to eat. If we want bread, we can pick up a sliced loaf within minutes. The ease and immediacy with which we get our food separates us from the people of the Bible. If they wanted bread, they had to plow the field, sow the seed, and pray for rain. If the rains came, they had to harvest the field, thresh the wheat, separate the wheat from the chaff, grind the seeds into flour, make the dough, and bake the bread. The labor intensiveness of survival meant they had little time for leisure.

The topography of the land of Israel prohibited farmers from a reliable source of water. They had to rely upon rain for their crops (Deut. 11:10–17). In the well-watered region of the Nile, the Egyptian farmers relied upon the flooding of the Nile to bring rich alluvial soil into their fields. The flat land allowed them to dig irrigation channels from the Nile to their fields. In the land of Israel, agriculture depended upon rain.

After a farmer went through the process of growing the wheat, harvesting it, and taking the seeds from the harvest, he faced a dilemma. He needed part of the seeds to feed his family; the other portion provided the seed for next year's crop. He had to divide the portion. When it came time to sow his seed for the next year, he didn't have the guarantee of rain. If he sowed seeds and rain didn't fall within a week, the seed he sowed was worthless. His only recourse was to take seed from the portion set aside for his family to eat. This is why droughts were so damaging to the world of the Bible. This is also why the farmer prayed for rain when he sowed the seed. Somehow, I doubt he prayed a weak prayer. He prayed with tears. Why? Because if God didn't send rain, the farmer and his family would have no food. You can imagine such a farmer kneeling in his field looking up into heaven and screaming, "Daddy, Daddy give us rain! If you don't, we are going to die!"

Israel's physical environment served as God's classroom. The children of Israel lived in the land based upon their obedience to Him. They survived in a land dependent upon rain by following the commandments of the One who sends rain. The confidence of the psalmist that "those who sow in tears reap with shouts of joy" stems from his confidence in a God who answers the cry of those in need. He doesn't leave us abandoned on the side of life's road.

The harsh environment of Israel forced the people to look to God as their source of provision and survival. Often in our world, things are easy, and we have a tendency to look to our own self-sufficiency. We don't honestly look to God as the source of our survival, and perhaps that's why our prayers are weak. The farmer in the field in Israel didn't have the luxury of self-sufficiency; his life depended upon God—and so does ours.

SCRIPTURE READINGS:

- Read Psalm 126 and James 5:7–18.
- Make a list of times when God answered your prayers or did something that was beyond your dreams and expectations.
- What prayers are you still patiently waiting for God to answer?
- What is God teaching you through the way He has answered (or through the waiting for an answer of) your prayers?

PRAYER

Thank You, Lord, for hearing and answering my prayers.

I praise You, God, for the great things You have done for me.

Hear my prayer and see my tears as I cry out fervently to You.

Respond to my requests, and may Your name be honored through me.

THE FAILURE OF SELF-RELIANCE

———

*If the L*ORD *does not build a house, its builders labored on it in vain. If the L*ORD *does not guard a city, its guards have kept watch in vain. It is in vain for you, that you rise up early and lie down late, that you eat the bread of anxious toil: so surely he gives his beloved ones (sound) sleep.*

PSALM 127:1–2

When I travel the ancient world, I'm often reminded of the poem "Ozymandias" by Percy Bysshe Shelley:

> I met a traveler from an antique land
> Who said, "Two vast and trunkless legs of stone
> Stand in the desert. Near them, on the sand,
> Half sunk, a shattered visage lies, whose frown,
> And wrinkled lip, and sneer of cold command,
> Tell that its sculptor well those passions read,
> Which yet survive, stamped on these lifeless things,
> The hand that mocked them, and the heart that fed:
> And on the pedestal these words appear:
> 'My name is Ozymandias, king of kings:
> Look on my works, ye Mighty, and despair!'
> Nothing beside remains. Round the decay
> Of that colossal wreck, boundless and bare
> The lone and level sands stretch far away."[3]

Shelley's poem refers to Ramesses II, one of the greatest pharaohs and builders of ancient Egypt. Of course the poem's theme is the futility of human effort in the face of time. All things decline and fade.

The psalmist captured a similar sentiment in Psalm 127: "If the LORD does not build a house, its builders labored on it in vain." The first verse of this wisdom psalm uses the images of a house and a guarded city; two images that evoked the preconditions for a happy and carefree life. Yet, the psalmist challenges that if God does not build the house and does not guard the city, all labor is in vain. Built houses and guarded cities, regardless of the human effort to build them and watch over them, will be for naught if the Lord is not a collaborator in the work.

Throughout history, humanity has congratulated itself on its achievements, assuming they will last for thousands of years. Traveling among ancient ruins as often as I do, I'm frequently confronted with the question: What will be left of our modern achievements in two hundred or a thousand years? Today people toil and labor to create lasting monuments to their lives and efforts while others simply live a life of happiness and ease. The psalmist doesn't encourage a slothful laziness that casts all responsibility upon God; rather, he understands that if we don't collaborate with God in our efforts, they won't last. The things we labor for to bring security, happiness, and carefree lives will fail if God doesn't labor with us. Ramesses II couldn't imagine a world where he was not a mighty king, but time moved on and consumed his efforts in the Egyptian sands.

Psalm 127 provides a picture of a successful, fulfilled life, and it all stems from perspective. The psalmist understands the toil and burdens of daily life, which is why his critique isn't on working for "bread" but on "anxious toil" (v. 2). The people imagined in verse 2 of the psalm aren't industrious people, but people who presume that nothing but toilsome work secures the sustenance of life and that only such work produces life's security. In such an attitude of self-reliance, they act, maybe even unconsciously, in a godless manner, even though they presume to believe in God. Their godlessness lies in their failure to acknowledge God at the heart of their daily labor. To those who are His beloved, God brings rest through sound sleep, which keeps the body and soul healthy.

The picture of the fulfilled life continues in verses 3–5, which speak about progeny. Children in the Bible, sons in particular, gave the family social power. So the psalmist encourages people to work hard to have children in their youth; he doesn't criticize those who seek these good things in life. His emphasis and perspective, however, is that these good things in life come because God is at work. Above all, these things only lead to a happy and fulfilled life when God is their source. This is the happy, successful, and satisfying life.

We live in a world consumed with anxious toil and arrogant self-reliance. Both sentiments fail to take account of God, the source of all. Psalm 127 provides an incredible perspective that only those things in which we collaborate with God will last. Even in our daily lives, He is at work and provides the bread we need and the children we have.

SCRIPTURE READINGS:

- Read Psalm 127; Ecclesiastes 2:18–26; and Matthew 6:19–21.
- What have been your biggest accomplishments or greatest successes?
- How do you feel when you accomplish an important task or have success at some endeavor?

- What type of work seems to last and what type of work seems temporary?
- How can you invest your energy in work that will last?

PRAYER

Lord, I pray that my work today will not be in vain.

Watch over my motives and guard my intentions.

May I invest my time, energy, and resources in work that will endure.

Bless Your name and those around me through my efforts today.

DAILY FAITH

———

Blessed is everyone who fears the LORD, who walks in His ways.

PSALM 128:1

Similar to Psalm 127, Psalm 128 provides a glimpse of daily life. It presents the life of good fortune as a consequence of the life lived in the fear of the Lord. Some may read this psalm and assume that nothing will bother those who follow the Lord; difficulties and trouble will remain far away. Others may read this psalm and assume that the psalmist ignored the troubles and difficulties that beset everyone, even those following the Lord. Both readings would be wrong. The beatitude formula used in verse 1 not only congratulates those who realize and live according to the program stated in the verse, but it also serves as an invitation to those who don't. It encourages them to consider the purpose of life and to understand that true blessedness doesn't exist outside of the fear of the Lord.

The biblical worldview is quite different from our modern worldview. Throughout the Bible, knowledge is acquired through the "fear of the LORD" (Ps. 128:1; Prov. 1:7; 9:10; 15:32; Job 28:28). For the psalmist, "everyone" can be part of those who fear the Lord; it wasn't a special status of election and revelation. Those who fear the Lord express a foundational trust in the goodness of God, who created the world and established Himself as the good and just judge. Because God is good, He causes the success of the person who fears Him. Knowledge, then, is acquired, according to the Bible, through an obedient relationship with the good and just Creator-Judge. It isn't something propositional, but relational. Moreover, the psalmist didn't assume that every moment of life would be great, but rather, that God, who is just, would act justly on behalf of those who obey Him.

Biblical poetry often uses a formula known as parallelism. It's a way of stating something at the beginning of a verse and then stating something either synonymously parallel or even antithetically parallel in the second half of the verse. In Psalm 128:1, we find parallelism between the phrases "everyone who fears the LORD" and "the ones walking in His ways." In other words, the poetry of the psalm identifies the meaning of "fearing the LORD"—"walking in His ways." The fear of the Lord, then, isn't merely an emotional response but a deep sense of awe that comes from submission to the Creator-Judge and His commandments. The evidence of fear of the Lord is obeying His commands or walking in His ways. The person who fears God seeks His Torah and loves to do and obey His commands; they walk in the paths of the Lord (Ps. 112:1; 119:1–3).

For people in Bible times, religion and faith weren't relegated to specific spheres of life. Religious practices, such as sacrifices, took place in a specified sacred area, but faith and religion filtered into everyday existence. Obedience to God (or the gods) had practical and tangible evidences in this life, here and now.

In the Old Testament, two practical evidences of obedience to God pertained to progeny and physical labor. For this reason, the psalmist describes how the person who fears the Lord is blessed—through fruitful labor and children (Ps. 128:2–4). For the people of the Bible, God's blessings penetrated the everyday existence of life. The Bible reminds people of God's interaction in the ordinary and calls those who aren't walking in His ways to come and partake of His blessings in day-to-day living.

If our faith can't be lived in the common and mundane existence of life, biblically speaking, it isn't a faith that takes God seriously. When people see our faith lived in practical ways, this serves as an invitation to come and submit to the ways of the Creator of the universe, to experience His goodness. The Jewish sages of Jesus' day often said, "It is as much a miracle that God provides our daily bread as that He parted the waters of the sea." Such an outlook sees the blessings of God in every aspect of life. It doesn't look for the extravagant miracle but understands that God's blessings rest in our labors and our families—"Thus shall the man be blessed who fears the LORD" (Ps. 128:4).

SCRIPTURE READINGS:

- Read Psalm 128 and Proverbs 15.
- What does it mean to "fear the LORD"?
- In what ways would others know that you "fear the LORD"?
- How does your obedience to God invite others to "walk in His ways"?

PRAYER

I ask You, Lord, to help me walk in Your ways.

May others see the benefits of fearing the Lord in my life.

Let me see Your blessings in the ordinary as well as in the extravagant.

Thank You for the practical and tangible ways You are at work in my life.

THE GOD WHO DEFENDS HIS PEOPLE

"Often have they attacked me from my youth"—let Israel now say—"often they have attacked me from my youth, yet they have not prevailed against me."

PSALM 129:1-2

From a certain standpoint, the existence of Israel is baffling. A small, nondescript nation, it was located along the most strategic highway of the ancient world, surrounded by larger, stronger, and more advanced nations. Yet these ancient super-powers—Assyrians, Babylonians, Persians, Greeks, and Romans—entered and exited from the world's stage while Israel remained. Israel's existence within this arena proved incredibly challenging, but nevertheless Israel survived. The Bible answers the reason for the existence of this small nation, and it stems from God's intimate relationship with them. He never discarded them, even when they disobeyed His commands. He remained faithful to His promises to their fathers Abraham, Isaac, and Jacob.

Psalm 129 represents a communal psalm that offers a dramatic picture of the fate of those who oppress Israel. Although the speaker used the first person singular "I" in verses 1 and 2, he included the collective Israel as the intended "I," which is made clear in the refrain "let Israel now say." The Bible frequently depicts Israel as a youth (Jer. 2:2; Ezek. 23:3, 8, 19, 21; Hos. 2:1; 11:1). When it speaks about Israel's youth, it often refers to the period of the Exodus in which Israel, beset with foes, relied upon the Lord to defend them and fight on their behalf (Ex. 23:20–23). In verses 1 and 2, the psalmist describes Israel's challenges from its youth of being attacked by its enemies. Still, Israel's enemies didn't prevail against it regardless of its small stature.

Although the psalmist didn't mention a yoke or goad used to harness animals and spur them to plow fields, his language, "The plowers plowed on my back," conjured in the minds of the ancient readers, where agriculture was preeminent, the images of a yoke and goad. This metaphor resonated with them as the image of a yoke was often used to describe the enslavement of a people to another. The entire act of plowing, including placing the yoke upon the back of the animal, acted as a metaphor for forced labor, oppression, submission to foreign rule, and slavery. (At times, enslaved people were actually put under the yoke and forced to pull a plow.) The psalmist used this metaphor to describe the enslaved position of Israel. It reflects a time of Israel's injury and devastation. Unlike in Psalm 128, where the person who fears the Lord reaps the benefit of their own labors, here the psalmist labors for an oppressor, which is why God's actions on Israel's behalf are so joyous.

Continuing with his metaphor of plowing a field, the psalmist reflects on God's righteous actions on behalf of Israel—"He has cut the cords of the wicked" (v. 4). In this context, "the cords of the wicked" refer to the cords that held the plow together, including the yoke. God acted on Israel's behalf and cut the cords of the oppressive plow.

The psalmist is looking back on what God has done in Israel's history. Israel's existence is explained by God's existence. What seems baffling to everyone else—why this nation continues to exist—is explained because the God of Israel, who is righteous, defends Israel from its enemies, those who hate Zion (v. 5). Israel's inexplicable existence derives from God's deliverance, because the blessing of the Lord is upon it (v. 8). The greater nations that surrounded Israel didn't experience such deliverance and preservation, which is why they passed out of history.

This psalm provides an incredible statement about God's ability to preserve His people in the midst of a challenging world filled with those who hate them. By weaving together strands of Israel's past, its suffering and divine deliverance, the psalmist makes a poignant statement about God's ability to preserve even the smallest of things in the midst of world powers. People could make similar comments about our smallness and lack of ability; we shouldn't be where we are. But "the LORD is righteous; He has cut the cords of the wicked."

SCRIPTURE READINGS:

- Read Psalm 129 and 1 Timothy 4:6–16.
- In what ways have you felt attacked, inferior, or put down recently, either by others or yourself?
- How did it make you feel or act in response?
- What does it mean to you that the Lord "has cut the cords of the wicked"?
- What gift(s) has God given you to be a blessing to others?

PRAYER

Lord, may I pay attention to Your voice, rather than to the voices of others.

Speak Your Word into my life.

Remove feelings of inferiority and inadequacy.

Let me be an example of love, faith, and purity.

THE GOD WHO HEALS

Out of the depths I cry to you, O LORD, my LORD, hear my voice;
let Your ears be attentive to the voice of my supplication for favor!

PSALM 130:1–2

The Bible grew from the soil of its world. Some things in the Bible can only be accurately understood with knowledge of the history, language, culture, and geography of the biblical world. But even those portions of the Bible that communicate easily across time, culture, and space gain an incredible depth and clarity when read in light of the ancient world of the Bible. The first two verses of Psalm 130 are like that.

When the psalmist proclaimed, "Out of the depths I cry to you," the depths he referred to literally mean "watery depths." This language layers two images within it. First, the "watery depths" refer to a natural phenomenon that occurs within the wilderness canyons of the land of Israel. To the east and south of the central hill country, rainwater that falls in the hills drains off into the dry land through deep canyons. This runoff creates raging torrents and flash floods that prove extremely dangerous (Ps. 124:1–5). As the terrain descends in elevation, these raging torrents become waterfalls that carve out pits at the bottom of the canyons. These pits fill up with silt and mire and prove treacherous to anyone caught in them (Ps. 40:2–3; 69:2–3, 15–16).

A person seeking to escape from the slimy clay of these pits would often be surrounded on three sides by steep cliffs. In this moment, the person would seek any foothold, even the tiniest one, in an attempt to escape. Even today, during the winter and spring when the rains fall in the hill country, hikers have to be extremely careful because they can find themselves caught suddenly in dangerous situations. At one level, the psalmist's mention of the "watery depths" conjures this image of great peril and the desperation of one caught in these treacherous waters.

To the ancient reader, mention of "watery depths" also brought to mind the "depths of the sea," which stood for the underworld (Sheol) and the chaotic and mythic primeval sea (Gen. 1:1–2; Isa. 51:10), which although it had been conquered by the Creator God still threatened creation and life. In this sense, the watery depths reflect the ancients' fear of death and the primeval chaos that threatened their existence. The cry from the depths evoked the distance that stood between the psalmist and the Lord (Jonah 2:3–7). His cry to the Lord looked across this chasm to the One who could save him from death and chaos. If we allow ourselves to look at the world through the eyes of the psalmist, we gain a much deeper sense of his pathos and his faith in the greatness of God.

No matter how deep the depths he was in, the psalmist remained confident that God would hear his cry and respond accordingly. Embedded within the psalmist's plea for God to hear his voice and be attentive to his supplications lies a statement of trust in the power and good will of God. A sincere cry to the Lord, regardless of the words and emotions, is a deep expression of faith because it assumes that One stands ready to hear the supplication who can and will answer.

Ancient Near Eastern prayer frequently included the motif of the "listening ears" of the gods. The petitioner sought to open the ears and hearing of the deity to their cry and trusted that the requests would be heard. This motif is represented in iconography from Egypt and Mesopotamia where people are depicted praying together with ears drawn in the picture symbolizing the supplicant's attempt to open the ears of their god. The biblical authors frequently referenced the ears and hearing of the Lord (Ps. 5:3; 10:17; 17:6; 31:3; 55:3; 61:2; 66:19; 71:2; 86:1, 6; 88:3; 94:9; 102:3; 142:7). In fact, the biblical authors contrasted how attentively the Lord listens to His people and quickly answers their cries as opposed to foreign gods and idols, who had no eyes to see, ears to hear, nor mouths to communicate (Ps. 115:6; 135:17).

This contrast appears most clearly in the duel between the God of Israel and Baal, the Phoenician storm god (1 Kings 18). Elijah ridiculed the prophets of Baal, who cried loudly to Baal from morning until noon, saying, "Cry aloud! Surely he is a god; perhaps he is busy with something else, or he is on a journey, or perhaps he is asleep and must be awakened" (v. 27). But there was "no voice, no answer, and no response" (v. 29). By contrast, the God of Israel answered immediately the brief prayer of Elijah (vv. 36–38). The God of Israel listens attentively and answers.

When the psalmist cries out to the Lord from the depths, he is aware to whom he cries: the God who listens and answers; the God who delivers the one threatened by the watery depths. This is the God to whom we pray.

SCRIPTURE READINGS:

- Read Psalm 130 and 1 John 1:5–2:6.
- How does it feel when you are talking to someone and they aren't really listening?
- If you could have the undivided attention of one famous or historical person, who would it be and what would you say?
- What does it mean to you to know that God "hears" and is "attentive" to your voice?
- What is the most important thing you want God to hear from you today?

PRAYER

Hear me, O Lord, as I cry for Your mercy.

You know my thoughts, my motives, and my actions.

Forgive me for my sins.

May my thoughts be true and my behavior be obedient to You.

Z E B
Cana
Nazareth
D

io   Itabyrins
S   A
   End
Esdraeli

Gaüra

harus
S   S   E
R   I
baste   Sabuure
Ebal M.
   Thirza
m v. Neapolis

   Phasaelis

lilo   Archelais

Bethaven
   Ephraim
   Bethanin
   Ma

Siloam

HUMBLE YOURSELF BEFORE THE LORD

O LORD, my heart is not arrogant and my eyes are not presumptuous, and I do not occupy myself with great things and with things that are too wonderful for me; Instead, I have calmed and quieted my soul.

PSALM 131:1–2

salm 131 is unique because the speaker is a woman: "like a nursed child with its mother, like the nursed child with me—so is my soul" (v. 2). This doesn't mean that a woman authored the psalm, but that the tone is the voice of a tender mother. This fits within the Old Testament tradition of women speaking prayers and psalms (Miriam in Ex. 15:21; Hannah in 1 Sam. 1:10–11; 2:1–10; Judg. 5:1–31; Ruth 4:14). In this psalm, the feminine voice brings tenderness to the moment of quiet calm before the Lord.

The ancient Israelites identified the heart as the center of one's ability to reason, know, understand, reflect, and judge. The eyes provided the portals through which a person saw the world and formed their views and opinions. Biblical authors frequently spoke of the heart and eyes as representing the centers of thinking and perceptions. The psalmist renounced the arrogance of the heart and the impudence of the eyes as prohibitive of coming before the Lord. His attitude parallels the thoughts in Proverbs: "Every heart that is arrogant is an abomination to the LORD. . . . The human mind plans the way, but the LORD directs the steps" (Prov. 16:5, 9).

A presumptuous, arrogant heart and proud, haughty eyes are two character traits the Bible routinely identifies with those who will be ultimately destroyed (Prov. 6:17–18; 16:18; 18:12; 21:4; 30:13). The Lord is against those with an arrogant heart and proud eyes, considering such attitudes sin (Isa. 2:11–17).

The psalmist said that he didn't have such attitudes. That was why he could come freely before the Lord. The psalmist's attitude parallels Job's attitude before God: "I know that You can do all things, and that no purpose of Yours can be thwarted. . . . I have uttered what I did not understand, things too wonderful for me, which I did not know. . . . I had heard of You by the hearing of the ear, but now my eye sees You; therefore, I give up and yet I am consoled—even in dust and ashes" (42:1–6). The encounter with God commands humility. Job contrasted the traditional knowledge of God, "I had heard of You by the hearing of the ear," with an experience of God that left him humbled and in awe, "but now my eye sees You." Job's experience with God transformed his perspective, so that even in dust and ashes he found consolation.

We live in a culture that endorses and markets arrogance and pride. We see it in athletics, government, media, and even in our churches—the cult of personality is everywhere. Yet, the Bible identifies haughtiness and pride as things that God hates because they place humans above Him. Arrogance fails to recognize that we are like the grass of the field, which is here today and gone tomorrow. Our lifespan and ability cannot match the vastness of time and space. But the One we serve can, and when we stand in front of Him and experience Him, pride and arrogance cannot abide. We find ourselves quieted at His greatness.

Some authors have suggested that Psalm 131:1 imitates a humbling prayer at the entrance of the temple precincts in which the petitioner examined his or her conscience, confessing trust in the Lord. If this is the case, it is interesting that ancient Israelites found themselves overwhelmed by awe at the greatness of God; it caused them to quiet and calm themselves. Could it be that our churches fail to provide opportunities for people to quiet and calm their souls, gazing at their finiteness in light of God's infiniteness? When ancient pilgrims approached the temple in Jerusalem, they did so with a sober and circumspect attitude that assessed the magnitude of the moment—they had come to stand before the Lord in His dwelling place upon the earth. This moment, although joyous, didn't cause them to respond with great noise or hysteria. In the midst of their journey, as they contemplated and humbled themselves, they found an inner peace and security, understanding that God, like the mother of a nursing child, protects and cares for His children.

SCRIPTURE READINGS:

- Read Psalm 131 and Psalm 46.
- What are the benefits of worshiping God with a "joyful noise"? (Ps. 95:1–2; 98; and 100:1–2)
- What are the benefits of worshiping God in "stillness" and in the "quiet places"? (Ps. 46:10 and Isa. 32:18)
- Which do you prefer? Why?
- What does it mean to humble yourself before God?

PRAYER

I humble myself before You, O Lord.

Quiet my heart and calm my mind with Your presence.

Keep me safe and give me Your peace today.

My hope is in You.

REMEMBER THE LORD

The Lᴏʀᴅ has chosen Zion; He has desired it for His habitation:
"This is my resting place forever; here I will reside,
for I have desired it."

PSALM 132:13–14

In the book of Exodus, the Lord commanded every able-bodied male to appear before Him three times a year. As the Israelites wandered in the wilderness, and even after they entered the land of Canaan, the Lord's sacred dwelling was a portable tent—the Tent of Meeting. David desired to build a permanent dwelling for the Lord in his new capital, Jerusalem (2 Sam. 7; Ps. 132), to consolidate the political and spiritual centers of the people of Israel. His son Solomon fulfilled this dream when he built the temple.

The Bible and archaeology both attest that the people continued to worship the Lord throughout the land of Israel outside of the temple in Jerusalem. Not everyone could make the journey to Jerusalem, so other temples and worship places dedicated to the God of Israel appeared throughout the land. In the eight and seventh centuries BC, two kings of Judah brought about religious and political reform that centralized the worship of the Lord in Jerusalem. Hezekiah and

Josiah tore down other places of worship, both for other gods and for the God of Israel, and made Jerusalem and its temple the center for worship. If any Israelite wanted to appear before the Lord, they had to journey to Jerusalem.

The reforms of Hezekiah and Josiah elevated Jerusalem as a political and spiritual center. Prior to their actions, Jerusalem was important, but their actions ensured that pilgrims would come from the four corners of the world to appear before the God who had chosen Jerusalem for His habitation. As Jews were dispersed throughout the world, Jerusalem remained the center of pilgrimage. Christians inherited the practice of pilgrimage from Judaism, which is why even today thousands of pilgrims come from all over the world to visit Jerusalem.

Psalm 132 weaves together David's desire to build a house for God and God's promise to build a house (dynasty) for David (2 Sam. 7). This psalm presents a special theology of Zion. As we have seen with other Pilgrim's Psalms (specifically 122 and 127), Jerusalem stood at the heart of biblical pilgrimage, not as a vacation destination, but as the dwelling place of God. As people journeyed there, they prepared themselves for the moment when they would arrive in the temple to appear before the Lord. It was a journey that required financial commitment as well as physical and spiritual commitment.

A person on a journey goes through a spectrum of emotions: anticipation, excitement, frustration, despair, anxiety, joy, and probably many others. Ancient pilgrims were no different. The Psalms of Ascent served to remind them of the process: the journey, the goal, and the joy that awaited them. At the same time, the psalms acted as a mirror to remind the pilgrims of their responsibility to be in the proper mindset as they appeared before the Lord.

In leading pilgrims and students through the land of Israel for a number of years, I'm often struck at some peoples' disappointment because the feelings they expected didn't materialize. They forget that travel, jetlag, new foods, and physical exertion all distract a person's focus from the purpose of their journey. I often tell groups that it's our responsibility as pilgrims to remember why we come: not for a feeling but to meet with the living God in His appointed land, in His appointed city. You don't have to travel to Israel to find yourself distracted from the goal of the journey. Life happens anywhere in the world, and it is messy. Many things serve to distract us. Perhaps this is why the psalmist of Psalm 132 begins, "O LORD, remember in David's favor all the hardships he endured," because by calling upon God to remember, it also reminds us of His promises and His faithfulness. In fact, throughout the Bible, we are called upon to remember, in part to make sure we don't get sidetracked on the journey.

SCRIPTURE READINGS:

- Read Psalm 132 and 2 Samuel 7.
- What has been your closest moment to God in the past few days?
- Describe the particular place, time, activity, or atmosphere where you feel God's presence most intensely.
- How do you prepare yourself for being close to God, for being in His presence?

PRAYER

Lord, I desire to be in Your presence.

Please draw me close as I remember the things You have done.

Let me find rest when I seek You.

Help me keep the promises I have made before You.

THE BLESSING OF UNITY

How very good and pleasant it is when kindred live together in unity. . . . It is like the dew of Hermon, which falls on the mountains of Zion. For there the LORD ordained His blessing, life forevermore.

PSALM 133:1, 3

Psalm 133 declares that the art of life is the art of community: "How very good and pleasant it is when kindred live together in unity." The final verse of the psalm identifies Zion as the place where the Lord established His blessing, which suggests that the psalmist intended the place where "kindred live together" to be identified as Zion, Jerusalem. It is certainly possible for people to "live together in unity" elsewhere in the world, but the psalmist isn't speaking about people getting along. He elevated Jerusalem, its inhabitants, and pilgrim visitors, as a model for "kindred" living together in unity, which for him included the spiritual experience of people coming to the temple.

The Bible emphasizes community living. People experienced God often as a community and not as individuals. From the standpoint of the Bible, sin's greatest impact was upon the community, not solely on the individual, which is why community units, like families, often bore the brunt of one person's sin. In this way, the biblical mind viewed familial and social relationships as primary conduits for a person's spiritual expression and experience.

The psalmist emphasized this point in verse 2, where he fused together two aspects of anointing. First, in the ancient world, people attending a celebratory banquet were often anointed with oil in order to create a sweet fragrance at the meal. The ancients used oil as perfume to cover up body odor and the smells of life. Second, oil was used to anoint important figures in the Bible. Priests, kings, and prophets were all anointed. When the high priest Aaron was anointed, the oil pouring over his beard and down his robe would have covered the ephod and breastplate that bore the names of the twelve tribes of Israel—a symbol of national unity. The dual images of oil being poured out emphasize the psalmist's message that God's blessings rest on the community that lives rightly together.

The geography of verse 3 is impossible. The dew of Hermon, which sits at the northern boundary of Israel, cannot fall on the mountains of Zion. This geographical impossibility has caused many to struggle with this verse. The issue, however, is not about geography but climate. Mount Hermon is the highest elevation in the land of Israel at over 9,000 feet above sea level. For much of the year, snow rests on its peaks. At the base of the mountain, two of the three headwaters that form the Jordan River appear from underground springs: the Dan and the Banias. As the snows of the mountain melt, the runoff flows through the region, finding its way into the Jordan River or the Sea of Galilee.

Quite simply, Mount Hermon represents the water sources of the land of Israel. Its region boasts incredible green, lush vegetation. Jerusalem, however, sits near the edge of the desert. Its ancient name, Zion, which the author of Psalm 133 used, comes from the word meaning "the dry place." While Jerusalem can receive rain during the winter months, it remains dry for much of the year. The contrast in the psalm focuses on wet, watery, and lush versus dry and barren. By contrasting the climates of these two regions within the land of Israel, the psalmist says that when people live rightly together in community it is as if the wet, life-giving waters of Hermon now reside on the mountains of Zion, the dry place.

Regardless of what brought ancient pilgrims to Jerusalem, whether a community festival or a personal need to appear before the Lord, when they arrived at the temple they found themselves among a community of people. Biblical worship within the temple was rarely private.

Life together can be messy. Quite often, modern spirituality focuses upon the individual and their relationship with God. It is highly self-centered and self-absorbed. But in the Bible, the primary way of experiencing God was with the community. What's more, God's blessings came upon the community that lived together rightly. I wonder how many of God's blessings and how much of His presence we forfeit because we fail to remember that when people live together in unity, there His blessing falls.

SCRIPTURE READINGS:

- Read Psalm 133 and Ephesians 4:1–16.
- Who are the most important people in your life?
- Why are they important to you?
- In what ways does God use them to bless your life?
- How can you bless those around you today?

PRAYER

Thank You, Lord, for the blessings of the people I love.

May I be attentive to the lessons they teach me.

Let me be a blessing to them today.

May Your name be honored in our lives.

THE MAKER OF HEAVEN AND EARTH

May the LORD, maker of heaven and earth, bless you from Zion.

PSALM 134:3

P salm 134 brings the Psalms of Ascent, the Pilgrim's Psalms, to conclusion. Verse 3, the concluding verse, represents a priestly blessing given to pilgrims as they prepared to return home. A theology of Zion runs throughout the Pilgrim's Psalms because the Lord dwelled in Zion. His presence drew pilgrims from the four corners of the earth; therefore, a blessing from Zion entailed "life" in the common everyday existence of familial happiness and nourishment, social and political peace, and communal prosperity. The Pilgrim's Psalms addressed these common levels of existence, and now the blessing of the Lord is invoked to bring life into the everyday existence of the traveler.

Making a pilgrimage to the temple in Jerusalem was a profound experience. The labor, financial commitment, time for the journey, and the sites of Jerusalem that awaited the pilgrims must have been incredible. But within the Pilgrim's Psalms, the pilgrims were reminded they cannot bask in the spiritual glory of the moment;

they must return home with the joy and blessing they encountered in the temple as part of their everyday, ordinary existence.

During the first century, pilgrims brought souvenir clay lamps home with them from Jerusalem. These lamps were manufactured in and around Jerusalem and have a distinctive spout. Archaeological excavations have uncovered them well outside of Jerusalem in areas like Galilee and the Golan. Even though artisans in these distant regions knew how to make these lamps, analysis of the clay indicates that all of these lamps came from the Jerusalem area. Pilgrims to Jerusalem brought the lamps back to their homes. The question has been asked why lamps, and the answer seems to be that the lamps provided an ongoing connection to the temple, where the lampstand, the menorah, stood. God is frequently identified with light, so the pilgrims sought to bring this symbol of the light of the temple and the light of God to their homes. They used these lamps to light their homes in the evening. This was a way to bring the holy experience of their pilgrimage into the mundane existence of their daily lives. When we bring our experiences with God into our daily lives, we find the mundane and ordinary elevated and sanctified.

The pilgrims couldn't remain in Jerusalem; they had to go back to their everyday lives. The blessing of Psalm 134 reminds the pilgrims that the God who dwells in Zion brings life to everyday existence. In this way, they must bring their experience with Him into the totality of their lives.

The ancient Israelites identified their God as the Maker of heaven and earth. Two thoughts are important here. First, in Psalm 134:3, the psalmist used the present participle form of the verb "make," which means that he viewed God in the continuing process of "making" the world ("May the LORD, the One making heaven and earth . . ."). This language demonstrates that the ancient Israelites viewed God as actively working in His creation. For them, He didn't simply create and then sit back and disengage from the world like a person winding a watch and letting it run on its own. For the psalmist, God remains actively involved in the work of creation; God is attentive to His creation. This forms a key characteristic of the biblical view of the God of the Bible.

Second, the blessing of Psalm 134:3 calls upon God, who is making the universe, to bless the pilgrim "from Zion." For the ancient Israelites, their God wasn't merely a creative force in the universe, but the God who acts in history. He was connected to time and space (Zion). In the Bible, He revealed Himself through His acts in history and in space, specifically the land of Israel. The ancient Israelites had a very intimate view of God; at times, this intimacy generated the emotion of fear as they encountered Him.

Among the sacred writings of the world's religions, the Bible alone presents a message tied to geography (space). The Bible acknowledges God as the universal Creator, but it connects Him to a people and a place. On the one hand, the psalms will declare that there is nowhere that we can run from His presence (Ps. 103); yet He dwells in Zion. This tie to geographical space brought the pilgrim on this journey to Jerusalem and to the temple.

As we have sought to universalize God, we have lost this key aspect felt by the authors of the Bible—the Creator of the universe dwells in Zion. The ancient pilgrims could have experienced God at their homes. The journey wasn't necessary, but through the journey—the preparation, the dangerous travel, the arrival in Jerusalem, and worshipping in the temple—the pilgrim was changed. Psalm 134 reminded the pilgrims to return home changed because of their experience of God in Zion, and to let this change affect the way they lived.

SCRIPTURE READINGS:

- Read Psalm 134 and 2 Corinthians 3:17–4:18.
- Why do you think God is described as "light"?
- What does it mean that God "continues to make" the heavens and the earth? (Ps. 134:3)
- In what ways is God continuing to make and transform you?
- Take a moment and listen for God's voice. What is He saying to you today?

PRAYER

I bless you, O Lord.

As I recognize all that You have done, speak to me.

Continue to make me and transform me, day by day.

From glory to glory, may Your name be praised.

LIVING AT THE CROSSROADS

---

*"Go forth from your native land and from your father's house
to the land that I will show you."*

GENESIS 12:1

ave you ever wondered why God led Abraham and his
descendants to the land of Israel and settled them there?
Why there? Why not somewhere else, like, say, Hawaii or
Switzerland? While this might seem a deeply theological question
to some, it really isn't. It's simply a question of geography. Look at
a map of the ancient Near East and notice the two great river civilizations. In the north between the Tigris and Euphrates, you see
the area known as Mesopotamia ("the land between the rivers"),
where the great civilizations of Sumer, Assyria, Babylon, and Persia
resided. To the south, along the Nile River, lay the great civilization
of Egypt, the land of Pharaohs. In the west of your map is the Mediterranean Sea, and south of Mesopotamia is the great Arabian Desert. Now, find the land of Israel on your map, and ask the question
again: Why this land?

Quite simply, the land of Israel provides the best navigable land bridge between the continents of Asia and Africa. It sits at the juncture of the two great river civilizations of Mesopotamia and Egypt, the land between the crossroads of the ancient world. Whoever controlled the land of Israel controlled international travel, communication, and commerce. Israel has never lived in isolation. It was a highly coveted piece of real estate in the ancient world. By virtue of its location, Israel's flora, fauna, and wildlife blend together the species and habitats of Africa and Asia. In a similar manner, the cultures of the major civilizations of the ancient world blended in the land of Israel. Throughout the Old Testament, this provided a challenge for the people of Israel.

So why this land? If you owned a business and wanted to let others know about it, where would you locate your advertisement? You would place it at the crossroads where the most people would see it. God placed Israel at the crossroads of the ancient world where they could be His greatest advertisement. The children of Israel didn't live in an isolated backwater, but at the place where cultures convened and collided. This provided Israel with incredible challenges because their ability to remain in the land depended upon their obedience to God (Deut. 8:7–20). Their ability to hold onto the land required their trust in God to sustain them at the crossroads.

Besides its strategic geographical significance, the land provided a classroom for God to reveal Himself to the children of Israel. The two great river civilizations in Egypt and Mesopotamia possessed developed cultures and religions. There was no place in those cultures for God to reveal Himself and teach Abraham and his descendants His ways. The land of Canaan didn't have such developed cultures and religions, and by taking Abraham and his children into this land—the crossroads—God had a better environment to teach them about trusting Him and to help them understand His uniqueness among all of the deities of the ancient Near East. Israel struggled at the crossroads; it wasn't easy. The outside influences affected Israel's trust in and obedience to God; yet He didn't let them isolate themselves. He wanted to reveal Himself to the world through the descendants of Abraham and His relationship with them.

When the Adversary came before God at the beginning of Job, God thrust Job into the arena to be seen by all. God put Job on display. In the land of Israel, Abraham and his descendants were on display, just as you and I are on display to our world today. God doesn't want us to isolate ourselves from the world. Yes, sometimes it's tough to live at the crossroads, but God still desires to reveal Himself to people and to teach them about Himself. Living at the crossroads requires that we trust God to sustain us. It also requires that we obey Him in order to demonstrate to the world who He is: "Let your light so shine before men, that they may see your good works and give glory to your Father who is in heaven" (Matt. 5:16).

SCRIPTURE READINGS:

- Read Genesis 12:1–9 and Matthew 5:13–16.
- What does "living at the crossroads" look like today?
- Think about your current situation (where you live, what you do, who you live among, the circumstances in your life) and describe the ways you have to trust in God to sustain you.
- What lessons is God teaching you through your current circumstances?

PRAYER

O Lord, I need your guidance today.

Lead me in Your ways.

Teach me to follow You and to look to You.

May others see who You are through my life.

Cana

Nazareth

Itabyrium

Endor

Esdrael

tharus

R I

ebaste Calliroe

Ebal M.

Thirza

em v.Nexpolis

Iulo Archelais

Betharene

Ephraim

Bethany

Siloam

ON WHOM DO YOU DEPEND?

For the Lord your God is bringing you into a good land, a land with streams and springs and fountains issuing from plain and hill; a land of wheat and barley, of vines, figs, and pomegranates, a land of olive trees and [date] honey.

DEUTERONOMY 8:7-8

The Bible repeatedly describes the land of Israel as "a land flowing with milk and honey"—a land that is good for the shepherd whose goats produce milk and a land good for the farmer who produces honey from the palm tree dates. Shepherds (pastoralists) and farmers (agriculturalists) formed two important social groups within the biblical world. The shepherd was a pastoral nomad who wandered in search of land to graze his flocks, living on the edge of the desert and settled society (Gen. 33:18). The farmer lived a more settled existence, planting and harvesting his crops. At times, tensions arose between shepherds and farmers (Gen. 4:11–16; 46:31–34); yet in other instances, farmers allowed shepherds to graze their flocks in harvested fields, which allowed good forage for the animals and fertilized the fields for the farmers (Gen. 37:12–17).

The Bible presents the Promised Land as a land that can sustain both the shepherd and the farmer, supporting flocks and agriculture. So, too, the Bible reflects the worldview of pastoralists and agriculturalists. The manner in which biblical people experienced God and expressed their spirituality grew out of their lives as shepherds and farmers. For this reason, biblical authors frequently used images from the lives of the shepherds and farmers to describe God, His message, and His relationship with humanity.

Even though the Bible describes the land of Israel as "a land flowing with milk and honey," a land good for shepherds and farmers, the land of Israel for the most part lacks an abundance of water, which created significant challenges for both the shepherd and the farmer. According to the book of Deuteronomy, God brought the Israelites into a land unlike Egypt and its river civilization; it was a land that God looked after (Deut. 11:10–12). Ancient Egyptians referred to the land of Canaan as "that poor country dependent on rain." In other words, in the land of Israel, the people had to depend upon God for their survival. In our modern era of Walmart, Sam's Club, and Costco, most of us can't grasp the deep connection the biblical person had to the land and the cycle of nature as the source of their existence. Whether they were a shepherd or a farmer, the life of an ancient person depended upon their ability to find pastures for flocks and to grow crops. Famines meant death to livestock, children, and the entire family. Such a tenuous existence created a natural dependence upon God to provide the right amount of rain for the grass and the crops. Living in this land, unlike the river societies of Egypt and Mesopotamia, taught the people to rely upon God as the source of their existence. Everything about the land of Israel made the people dependent upon God to sustain them.

The Israelites celebrated the fall Feast of Tabernacles (Succot) as a time when the people entreated God to send rain. Their dependence upon God for rain was a need He exploited whenever the people sinned. As a means of turning their hearts back to Him, He would withhold rain, "shutting the heavens" (Deut. 11:13–17; Amos 4:7–8; Isa. 5:6; Jer. 14:4; 2 Chron. 6:26).

The psalmist described the relationship between God and His people when he penned, "The LORD is my shepherd." Biblical readers understood that sheep depend entirely on the shepherd to keep them alive by finding places for them to pasture and by protecting them from enemies and threats. The shepherd found places of nourishment and safe places for the sheep to walk. Without the guidance of the shepherd, the sheep would die.

Often modern readers find themselves disconnected from the world of the Bible, its time and place. In our modern Western society of self-made individuals, we often forget what dependence upon God truly means. The land of Israel served as God's schoolhouse for the children of Israel. In that land, God taught them lessons of trust, obedience, and reliance upon Him. Sometimes we have a tendency to overly spiritualize the Bible and God's working in our lives. The realities of the land that flowed "with milk and honey" created a genuine dependence upon God for the children of Israel. He still wants us to trust Him and depend upon Him every day.

SCRIPTURE READINGS:

- Read Deuteronomy 8 and Psalm 23.
- How is God like a shepherd? What characteristics come to mind?
- Describe a time when you had to trust completely in God's provision. How did God lead you through that situation?
- Where is God leading you today?
- In what ways do you need to trust and depend on Him?

PRAYER

Lord, You are my shepherd.

Protect me and provide for my needs.

Keep me from straying away from the safety of Your care.

Help me to trust and obey You today.

Z. E. B
Cana
Nazareth
M.
Itabyr
io
S. Ze.
Endo
Esdrael.
Cana
harus
S. S. E
R Y
baste Sala
Ebal M.
Thirza
em v. Neapolis
Masaba
Jule Archelais
Bethaven
Ephron
Bethania
M.
A.
Siloam

95

ΑΙΝΩΝ ΕΝΘ
ΝΥΝ Ο CΑΠCΑ
ΦΑC

ΒΕΘΑΒΑΡΑ
Τ ΟΤ ΥΑΓΙΥ ΙΩΑΝ
ΤΥΒΑ   ΠΤΙCΜ
ΤΟC

ΑΤΟΚΑΙΤ   ΑΛΩΝΑΤΑΘΗ
ΝΙΘΟΝ   ΒΗΘΑΓ

ΙΕΡΙΧΩ
ΑΓΙ
ΛΙΟΥ

THE DESERT, GOD'S CLASSROOM

Remember the long way that the LORD your God has led you . . .
in the wilderness, in order to humble you, testing you to know what
was in your heart, whether or not you would keep His command-
ments. He humbled you by letting you hunger, then by feeding
you with manna . . . in order to make you understand that one
does not live by bread alone, but by every word that
comes from the mouth of the LORD.

DEUTERONOMY 8:2–3

T he children of Israel began life in the wilderness as pasto-
ralist nomads. Their three greatest leaders in the Old Testament, Abraham, Moses, and David, were all shepherds. They
came from the dry wilderness, and even in the land of Israel they
sat precariously on the edge of the desert, a land that constantly
depended upon the rains of heaven (Deut. 11:10–12). This deep
connection to the desert, the dry wilderness, also made the desert
God's classroom for His people, teaching them and testing whether
or not they would trust Him and obey His commandments.

The desert teaches two principal things: humility and hospitality. The Bible tells us that Moses, the shepherd, was the most humble of all men (Num. 12:3). In the wilderness there are no self-made people or Lone Rangers. You can't survive in the desert on your own; on your own, you die. Pastoralists rely on what little grass grows in the desert from the winter rains. Rainfall, however, is not evenly distributed, so the grass is not evenly distributed. If shepherding nomads like the Israelites find green grass, the flocks flourish and the people survive, but if there is a famine or they don't find grass, the flocks perish and the people die (Gen. 12:10; 26:1). For this reason, those who shepherd in the desert have to save in the good years for the lean years that will surely come.

They must live humbly, which is why in the desert everyone has the same standard of living. This is apparent in their tents, which are all the same size, made of the same cloth, and bear the same interior decoration; everyone wears the same clothes. No one lives more ostentatiously than another or flaunts the family wealth.

The desert is a great equalizer. While a nomadic shepherd may find green pastures for his flocks this year, he may not in subsequent years. In the years of want, he must depend upon his neighbors. If he lived as a self-made person during the years of plenty, flaunting his wealth, he would find himself alone and swallowed by the desert in his time of want. Desert dwellers understand how quickly fortune can turn, so within desert culture, no one looks down on the one who presently doesn't have because each one's situation can quickly change. Next year they might be the one who is in need.

The desert breeds humility for survival. A person doesn't find green pastures based upon their intelligence or powers. In the desert, a person learns of their need for God and others; one can't become arrogant in the desert and live.

It is this realization of the need for others that creates the desert culture of hospitality. Shepherding nomads live with their flocks. They obtain meat and milk from the animals and they sell them at market. Taking the flocks to the markets can prove an arduous task, for the market may be a long distance (sometimes hundreds of miles) from where the shepherd lives. So, too, in order to find well-watered pastures, shepherds will travel away from their families and flocks to find the watered lands. Traveling alone in the desert places a person in great danger. Bandits, animals, and dried-up watering holes are serious threats to survival. Even the smallest things pose grave threats in the desert.

This is why every tent is a place of refuge and rest. Those who live in the desert show hospitality to travelers, even to complete strangers. Any traveler can find food, hospitality, and lodging in a desert tent without question. Within the Bedouin (Arab desert-dwellers) culture, a stranger is permitted lodging for three days without question (even asking their name) or payment. Those living in the desert understand the need to show hospitality because one day they, too, will need it. Hospitality is valued as an honor, particularly an opportunity to honor God.

Abraham's hospitality and generosity (Gen. 18) demonstrate the depth to which he learned the lesson of hospitality within the dry wilderness. We live in a world and culture consumed with self and rugged individualism. Arrogance abounds, even among many Christian leaders. In the lives of the children of Israel, the desert functioned as God's classroom to teach them dependence upon Him. It also sensitized them to their need of others and to their need to help others. The Bible characterized its ideal leaders as those who learned the lessons of the desert. I wonder, what do we allow God to teach us when He leads us into the desert?

SCRIPTURE READINGS:

- Read Deuteronomy 11; Genesis 18:1–15; and 1 Peter 4:1–11.
- What do you think of when you read the statement: "The desert is the great equalizer"?
- When have you felt you were in a "desert" (emotional, spiritual, relational, etc.) and what lessons did you learn?
- Describe a time when the hospitality and generosity of others helped you through a desert experience.
- How have you helped others through your generosity or made them feel welcomed by your hospitality?

PRAYER

Lord, keep me from being so self-reliant and self-concerned that I don't see the needs of those around me.

Help me to be generous and hospitable to others.

Because I have received grace, let me be gracious today.

WHO IS YOUR GOD?

"Now summon all Israel to join me at Mount Carmel, together with the four hundred and fifty prophets of Baal and the four hundred prophets of Asherah who eat at Jezebel's table."

1 KINGS 18:19

M any people mistakenly assume that the children of Israel routinely abandoned the worship of Yahweh completely to worship other gods like Baal and Asherah. While some invariably turned their backs on God, the major problem the prophets faced was the desire of the children of Israel to "cover all their bases." Yes, they would worship Yahweh, but they would *also* worship Asherah, a female fertility goddess, or Baal, the storm god (Jer. 7:9–20), just to make sure they were covered in times of crisis. The God of Israel, however, routinely described Himself as "a jealous God" (Ex. 20:5; 24:13; Deut. 4:24; 5:9; 6:15; 32:19, 21; Josh. 24:19), One who refused to share the love and devotion of His people with anyone else.

During the reign of King Ahab (eighth century BC), Baal worship competed with the worship of Yawheh within the northern kingdom of Israel. Ahab married a Phoenician princess, Jezebel, who encouraged the worship of Baal and his female consort, Asherah (Baal worship originated along the Phoenician coast). Because people of the northern kingdom of Israel accepted the worship of Baal and Asherah, God sent a drought on the land, a grand statement about the impotence of the storm god, Baal. God's principal spokesperson to King Ahab and the people was the prophet Elijah. After spending some time in hiding from Ahab, Elijah returned to challenge Ahab, Baal, the prophets of Baal, and the children of Israel with the question, "Who indeed is God?" in a dramatic confrontation upon Mount Carmel.

The biblical author of Kings doesn't explain Elijah's motivation for staging this confrontation on Mount Carmel because he assumes that the reader understands the geographic significance and dynamic of this clash. Unfortunately, modern readers are not attuned to the geo-political importance of Mount Carmel within the kingdom of Israel so they fail to capture the significance and statement Elijah made by selecting Mount Carmel.

Mount Carmel doesn't have a singular peak; rather, it's a ridge of hills that bisects the Plain of Sharon jutting out into the Mediterranean Sea and outlining the southwestern boundary of the Jezreel Valley. Its geographic location along the coast of Israel, as well as its altitude, means that it has some form of precipitation approximately 250 days a year. Moreover, during the Old Testament period, Mount Carmel formed the southern boundary between the northern kingdom of Israel and Phoenicia, the home of Jezebel and the birthplace of Baal worship.

Elijah called for this confrontation after an extended drought. Baal, the storm god, was worshiped on high places like Mount Carmel (1 Kings 18:26). The frequent precipitation on Mount Carmel offers the best opportunity for the storm god to break the drought; moreover, Mount Carmel's location along the border of Phoenicia where Baal worship originated was deemed an appropriate setting for

Baal to display his power. To use the modern sports analogy, Baal had home-court advantage. Elijah had to face a hostile crowd; he even had to repair the altar of the Lord (v. 30).

The author of Kings contrasts the hysteria of the prophets of Baal against the calm confidence of Elijah. In fact, the hysteria of the prophets of Baal further underscores the impotence of Baal, as Elijah pointed out with his taunts (1 Kings 18:27). By contrast, the God of Israel is never impotent or at a disadvantage. Elijah's brief prayer and God's immediate response contrasts with the long, drawn-out frenzy of the worshippers of Baal who wasted themselves most of the day and received no answer.

We live in a world that seeks to shrink our view of God: "Has God really said?" "Is God really the way He presents Himself in the Bible?" Our culture doesn't demand that we turn our backs on God, but we too often seek to cover our bases, just in case. The issue is quite similar: "Who indeed is God?" The irony is that sometimes our churches look more like the hysteria of the prophets of Baal trying to entice God into acting and answering, when what we desperately need in our churches and our lives is the quiet confidence of Elijah, where we can say, "The LORD, He is God" (1 Kings 18:39).

SCRIPTURE READINGS:

- Read 1 Kings 18.
- In what ways do we "cover all our bases" today?
- Make a list of things that we trust in besides (sometimes before) God.
- What made the difference between Elijah's prayer and those of Baal's prophets on Mount Carmel?

PRAYER

O Lord, God of Abraham, Isaac, Israel, and Elijah, make Yourself known to me.

I am Your servant and I trust Your Word.

Answer my prayer so that others will know of your divine power.

You are the Lord, You are God, and there is no one like You.

IN WHAT DO YOU TRUST?

"Be sure to set as king over yourself one of your own people. . . .
Moreover, he shall not keep many horses."

DEUTERONOMY 17:15–16

The book of Deuteronomy outlines the law of the king (17:14–20) in which the king is not to keep many horses, have many wives, or amass silver and gold to excess. According to the author of Kings, King Solomon violated each of these mandates. He had many foreign wives (1 Kings 11:1–6); he accrued excesses of silver and gold (10:23–25, 27); and he amassed a force of horses and chariots that he stationed "in the chariot towns" (v. 26). Although the book of Kings doesn't specify the location of the chariot towns, it lists three significant cities that Solomon fortified: Hazor, Megiddo, and Gezer (9:15).

These three cities guarded the international coastal highway that ran through the land of Israel, connecting Egypt in the south with the Mesopotamian kingdoms in the north. This was the most important highway in the Old Testament world. Israel's strategic location along this highway shaped much of its history and existence. Solomon's fortification of Hazor, Megiddo, and Gezer indicates that his kingdom exercised influence along this important international highway.

The strategic location of these cities along this highway makes Hazor, Megiddo, and Gezer prime candidates as the "chariot towns" and "cavalry towns" (1 Kings 9:19; 10:26) of Solomon. Horses and chariots provided a strategic and technological advantage in ancient warfare, and whoever could exert control along the international highway affected international commerce, communication, and movement. Excavations at Megiddo have uncovered several building phases of horse stables, indicating that, in fact, Megiddo was fortified as a "chariot town" and "cavalry town." Not only did Megiddo guard the international coastal highway, it also watched over the western entrance into the fertile Jezreel Valley, in which north-south roadways converged with east-west roadways, making it supremely important for the kingdom of Israel. Excavations have revealed that certain phases of the horse stables date to the time of King Ahab, who ruled the northern kingdom of Israel in the eighth century BC.

Once we understand the geographic significance of Israel and its place along the international coastal highway and the strategic significance of Megiddo to guard Israel's interests along this highway, we can grasp why Megiddo became a town of chariots and horses. We can also understand why the kings of Israel were drawn to build up chariot and cavalry forces at strategic sites like Megiddo. This ensured the safety of the kingdom. These forces placed Israel on equal military and technological footing with the kingdoms around it, protecting its existence in the land. Having horses and chariots provided a political security and a sense of well-being to the rulers of Israel. It also made their kings as powerful as the kings around them, giving them added prestige (Isa. 37:24). The only problem, however, from the standpoint of the biblical authors, was that Israel's existence in the land depended solely upon God and the people's trust in Him.

The prophet Isaiah chastises those who hoped in the military strength of horses: "Ha! Those who go down to Egypt for help, and they rely upon horses! They have put their trust in abundance of chariots, in vast numbers of riders, and they have not turned to the Holy One of Israel; they have not sought the Lord" (Isa. 31:1; Mic. 1:8–16). The psalmist contrasts those relying upon horses and chariots with those who hope in the Lord: "They call on chariots, they call on horses, but we call on the name of the LORD our God" (Ps. 20:7).

Trusting in God is a tricky thing. Israel's geographic setting underscored its need to trust in God, as well as the temptation to rely upon contemporary technology to keep them in the land God had given them. Was it wrong for them to build up horse and chariot forces? Of course not. The problem came when the political rulers of Israel and Judah relied upon military technology to protect them rather than turning to God and trusting Him to keep them in the land.

We live in an increasingly changing and challenging world. The events of recent years have shown the fragility of governments, corporations, financial institutions, individuals, and leaders. Daily, new technologies make last year's technologies obsolete. Where does trusting God fit in our rapidly evolving and turbulent world? Our world has made us dependent upon technology and ourselves to the extent that we can easily buy into the illusion of our own power, as individuals, countries, corporations, and even churches. The political message of the prophets serves as a dire warning to remember where the source of trust must lie: Beware of relying upon horses!

SCRIPTURE READINGS:

- Read Deuteronomy 17:14–20; 1 Kings 9:1–19; and Psalm 20.
- Make a list of modern conveniences that most people couldn't live without.
- What people, things, or circumstances do you depend upon for your safety, security, and satisfaction?
- What does "trust in the name of the Lord our God" look like in today's modern world?

PRAYER

I know that the Lord saves those who trust in Him.

Lord, answer me when trouble comes my way.

Send help and give me support.

Grant the desire of my heart and have Your way in me.

THE GOD OF THE DOWNTRODDEN

———

*Then the word of the L*ORD *came to Elijah the Tishbite: "Go down and confront King Ahab of Israel, who resides in Samaria. He is now in Naboth's vineyard; he has gone down there to take possession of it."*

1 KINGS 21:17–18

I f you asked most people "What is a prophet?" and "What is prophecy?" they would probably answer something to the effect that a prophet is a person who predicts or foretells the future and prophecy is what a prophet does in foretelling the future. For many Christians, prophets and prophecy principally have to do with fore-telling things to come. In the Bible, however, prophets did very little predicting of the future; rather, they served as God's mouthpiece, delivering His messages to people, "Thus says the LORD."

The biblical prophets had far more to say about political, religious, and social issues than they did about the future. The prophets challenged the peoples' religious commitment to God (1 Kings 18). They challenged Israel and Judah's reliance upon foreign governments and military strength (Isa. 31:1), and they challenged the social abuses within ancient Israelite society. They spoke for God, challenging the rich and powerful to listen to the voice of the down-trodden. They faced down political rulers, declaring that even the king is not above God's law. They called for Israel to be socially conscious. Even Jesus understood His prophetic task as giving voice to the needs of the poor and downtrodden (Luke 4:16–30).

The motivation of the prophet's social message was not philan-thropy or trendy causes; rather, the prophet understood that the God of Israel was the defender of the widow, orphan, and for-eigner—those who had no advocate in the ancient world. The prophet realized that God identified with the needs of the poor and downtrodden and saw the abuse of riches and power as an abomination (Amos 2:6–8; 4:1–3; 5:10–24). The story of Naboth's vineyard (1 Kings 21) highlights the social message of the proph-ets. Unable to get Naboth to part with his ancestral land, Jezebel schemed to have Naboth falsely accused so her husband, Ahab, could take possession of Naboth's land. Such injustice provoked God to send Elijah to confront the king and queen and to render God's judgment upon them for their wicked act, which eventually resulted in their deaths.

In the nineteenth century, the fascination of liberal protestant churches with a social gospel generated a reaction among other Christians against anything that smacked of such an ideology. The problem, however, as with many reactionary movements, was that people turned too far away from a social message. Today, our modern culture is inundated with social causes; they've become a trendy part of Western society. Unfortunately, we often fail to ascertain the role of the biblical prophets as the voice of God speaking to the political, religious, and social abuses within a society. Paul mentioned in Ephesians that God has given gifts to the church, including the gift of prophets (4:7–16). The message of the biblical prophets answered in the affirmative that, indeed, I am my brother's keeper. It was a message they spoke to the rich and powerful of their day—a message they shouted before the king because they realized that the Spirit of the Lord had anointed them to address the plight of the downtrodden, to bring His hope to those who had none (Isa. 61:1–3).

SCRIPTURE READINGS:

- Read 1 Kings 21; Isaiah 58; and Luke 4:16–30.
- Who are the "downtrodden" and victims of social abuses today?
- How can Christians, followers of God, be a voice for those who have suffered from social injustice?
- God's message of hope is often best communicated person-to-person and face-to-face. Whom can you encourage today with God's message of hope?

PRAYER

May the Spirit of the Lord anoint me today.

Let me speak the good news to those that need to hear it most.

Use me to bring healing, freedom, and comfort to those who suffer.

May Your name be glorified and exalted through me.

THE SOVEREIGN GOD

So Joseph went after his brothers, and found them at Dothan.
GENESIS 37:17

He said, "Go and find where he is; I will send and seize him."
He was told, "He is in Dothan."
2 KINGS 6:13

The village of Dothan sits in a small valley, the Dothan Valley, separated by a line of hills in the north that form the large Jezreel Valley. The most important international highway of the ancient world, which connected Egypt with Damascus and Mesopotamia, passed through the land of Israel. Much of the highway passed along the coast, but it turned inland heading northeast towards Damascus due to the mountainous terrain of the Carmel Range and the Upper Galilee. This international highway entered the Jezreel Valley through three passes in the Carmel Range. The southern pass took travelers through the Dothan Valley.

Dothan is the setting for two different stories in the Bible. In the book of Genesis, Joseph sought his brothers in the area of Dothan where they had gone to pasture their flocks. It was here that his brothers threw him into a pit and sold him to traders following the international coastal highway traveling to Egypt (Gen. 37:17–36). Joseph, then, found himself a slave in Egypt where the wife of his master, Potiphar, falsely accused him, so he ended up in prison (39:1–23).

The second story comes from the life of Elisha the prophet. During a war with Israel, Elisha thwarted the plans of the king of Aram by warning the king of Israel against the plans of the king of Aram. The king of Aram searched for Elisha and found him living at Dothan; so the king sent horses and chariots to surround the city and capture Elisha (2 Kings 6:8–14). When Elisha's servant arose and went out in the morning, he found them surrounded by the Arameans. Fearfully asking his master what to do, Elisha prayed that God would open the servant's eyes that he might see (v. 17). So the Lord opened the servant's eyes, and he saw the hills around Dothan filled with horses and chariots of fire. When the Arameans attacked, Elisha prayed, and God struck them with blindness. Elisha then took the blinded Arameans to Samaria, the capital of the kingdom of Israel, and the king of Aram ceased raiding Israel (vv. 17–23).

Most of us love the story of Elisha and the chariots of fire because we recite stories of God's deliverance in order to encourage our faith. Yet Joseph's story in Dothan is not one of deliverance. Did he lack faith? Were there no "chariots" for Joseph because he sinned or didn't trust God enough? Joseph's experience at Dothan was quite different from Elisha's. As much as Elisha's story encourages us, Joseph's tale troubles us because there is no absolute answer to the question, "Why do bad things happen to good people?"

The difference between the stories lies in God's sovereignty. You see, if God had not taken Joseph from the land of Canaan, a young man upon whom His Spirit resided, the future of the nation of Israel would have been in doubt. God knew Israel's survival depended upon the storehouses of Egypt during seven years of famine. Of course, Israel's sojourn in Egypt not only saved Jacob and his children, but it also enabled God's deliverance years later through the agency of Moses. The story of God's deliverance of Israel from Egypt became the central narrative of God's redemption in the minds and history of the Jewish people. But had there been no pit in Dothan, there would have been no salvation from famine and deliverance from Egypt.

The two stories of Dothan illustrate that if we serve God, we accept that He can do whatever He wants. We can trust Him because He is good. He can deliver with chariots of fire, but at times, He must take us through the pit to get us to the palace. In spite of difficult circumstances, Joseph chose to remain obedient and faithful to God. I'm sure that in the pit, as a slave, and in prison, Joseph wrestled with doubts, but God worked His purposes and brought salvation and redemption because Joseph remained faithful.

SCRIPTURE READINGS:

- Read Genesis 37:12–36 and 2 Kings 6:8–23.
- Does the statement, "If there is no pit in Dothan (for Joseph), there is no salvation from famine and deliverance from Egypt (for Israel)" encourage or discourage you? Why?
- Describe a time when God provided an Elijah-type deliverance for you. What did you learn?
- Describe a time where God seemingly put you through a "Joseph-type" or "in-the-pit" experience. What did you learn?

PRAYER

O Lord, let me see that You are with me.

Whether it is in the pit or with mighty chariots, You are with me.

Keep me safe and continue to teach me to be obedient to You.

No matter the circumstances, accomplish Your purposes through me.

GOD, OUR FATHER

"Our Father in heaven . . ."

MATTHEW 6:9

We find the idea of God as Father throughout the Old Testament. We find people named Abiyah or Abiyahu meaning "Yahweh is (my) Father" (Hosea 11:1; Jer. 31:9, 20; Isa. 63:15; 64:8; Ps. 68:5; 103:13; 89:26). By identifying God as Father, the biblical writers highlight the close relationship between God and His creation and that we, as His creation, have a responsibility to obey Him and follow His ways (Deut. 32:6; Mal. 1:6).

This characterization continued and grew within first-century Judaism, the time of Jesus. Within ancient Jewish prayers, people routinely addressed God as the Father in heaven. Certain pious individuals often referred to God as Father and described their relationship with Him as that of a father to a son. Once, during a drought, the sages of Israel sent children to ask Abba Hilkia, a pious individual, to pray for rain. The children tugged on his cloak begging, "Father, Father [Abba, Abba] give us rain!" Abba Hilkia prayed, "Ruler of the universe, do this for those who do not distinguish between a Father [Abba] who can give rain and a father [Abba] who cannot." During a time when Judaism was undergoing a great crisis, the question was asked, "On whom can we stay ourselves?" The response came, "On our Father in heaven."

Jewish parables frequently portrayed God as the father of a household (Matt. 21:28–32; Luke 15:11–32). In one parable, the sages illustrated God's passionate concern for Israel by describing the love of a father for a wayward child: "To what may this matter be compared? To the son of a king who took to evil ways. The king sent a tutor to him who appealed to him saying, 'Repent my son.' The son, however, sent him back to his father [with the message], 'How can I have the impudence to return? I am ashamed to come before you.' Thereupon his father sent back to him, 'My son, is a son ever ashamed to return to his father? And is it not to your father that you will be returning?'" In another parable, God's pursuit of the lost is described, "The matter may be compared to the son of a king who was far away from his father—a hundred days' journey. His friends said to him, 'Return to your father!' He replied, 'I am not able.' His father sent him a message, 'Come as far as you are able according to your own strength, and I will come to you the rest of the way!'"[4]

These parables parallel Jesus' primary description of God as Father. In fact, Jesus' recognition of God as Father formed the foundation of His entire worldview. All of Jesus' teachings can be summarized in the simple word *relax*. Why? Because we have a Father in heaven who knows what we need (Matt. 6:25–34)—who rushes to find those have gone astray while they are still on the road (Luke 15:11–32)—so relax and don't worry. Moreover, if we who are evil know how to take care of our children, how much more so will God, our Father in heaven, take care of us (Matt. 7:7–11). The prayer Jesus taught His disciples to pray (6:9–13) stands upon the conviction that the One we address is "our Father in heaven."

Jesus not only viewed God as the Father of the "elect" or "chosen," but of all people whether righteous or not: "Love your enemies and pray for those who persecute you, so that you may be sons of your Father who is in heaven; for he makes his sun rise on the evil and the good, and sends rain on the just and on the unjust" (Matt. 5:44–45). According to Jesus, no person or group has exclusive rights to God and His mercy; everyone is His creation.

We live in a world consumed with worry, tension, and strife between races, nationalities, and religions. In such a world, Jesus reminds us to relax, because our Father in heaven loves and care for us. Jesus also reminds us to love even those who hate us because that same Father "causes His sun to rise on the evil and the good."

SCRIPTURE READINGS:

- Read Matthew 6:9–13, 25–34; 21:28–32; and Luke 15:11–32.
- What thoughts and emotions does the idea of God as your heavenly Father bring to your mind?
- If we are God's children, how does that affect our relationship with our "Father in heaven"?
- How does God, as Father, model for us how to parent our children?

PRAYER

Heavenly Father, thank You for Your love.

You know what I need before I ask.

Even when I am far from home, You come to my rescue.

Help me to bring honor to Your name.

SANCTIFYING GOD'S NAME

"May Your name be sanctified . . ."

MATTHEW 6:9

The usual English translation of the first petition of the Lord's Prayer, "Hallowed be your name," fails to capture the meaning of the phrase intended by Jesus, which was "May Your name be sanctified." In the Old Testament, God's name is sanctified by how He acts (Isa. 6:3). The prophet Ezekiel declared, "I [God] will display my greatness and my holiness [literally, I will make myself great and sanctify myself] and make myself known in the eyes of many nations; then they will know that I am the LORD" (38:23). The idea that God's actions sanctify His name appears in a Jewish prayer: "May Your name be magnified, sanctified, and exalted, our King, for every drop that you send us."

God's name is also sanctified, according to the Bible, by how His children act. In the book of Numbers, God instructed Moses to speak to the rock in order for the children of Israel to receive water. However, Moses struck the rock, causing water to issue forth. The Lord responded to Moses and Aaron, "Because you did not trust me, to treat me as holy [literally, to sanctify me] before the eyes of the children of Israel, therefore, you will not enter with this assembly into the land that I gave to them" (Num. 20:12). Moses' disobedience failed to sanctify God's name, which assumes that his obedience would have sanctified God's name. The prophet Amos likewise saw that Israel's disobedience failed to sanctify God's name but, rather, profaned it: "For three transgressions of Israel and for four, I will not revoke the punishment; because they sell the righteous for silver, and the needy for a pair of sandals—they trample the head of the poor into the dust of the earth and push the afflicted out of the way; father and son go into the same girl, so that My holy name is profaned" (Amos 2:6–7).

A Jewish sage by the name of Rabbi Shimon ben Eleazar succinctly articulated the idea that God's name is at stake in His people: "Whenever Israel does the will of the Omnipresent, then His name is magnified in the world, but whenever Israel does not do His will, His name is profaned in the world." Within the Old Testament and ancient Jewish piety, God's name is sanctified in the common ordinary actions of life, especially in the way we treat others, including those outside our circles. Later Jewish sages forbade any unethical economic dealings with Gentiles lest "the name of heaven be profaned among the nations."[5] Paul, likewise, called upon the Jews of Rome to live holy lives in the midst of Gentiles lest the name of the Lord be profaned among the Gentiles (Rom. 2:21–24).

From ancient Judaism to the present day, Jewish suffering and death as a result of one's obedience to God and His commandments was referred to as "the sanctification of the Name," which became a euphemism for the act of martyrdom—dying because of one's devotion to God's commands. In other words, a person's devotion and obedience to God could in fact lead to death, and this devotion was the ultimate act of sanctifying God's name in this world.

A Jewish prayer predating the time of Jesus known as the Kedusah, or "sanctification," beseeches the Lord, "May we sanctify Your name in this world as it is sanctified in the highest of heaven." This prayer parallels Jesus' benediction, "May Your name be sanctified. . . . May Your will be done on earth as it is in heaven." When Jesus taught His disciples to pray, the first request focused upon the sanctification of God's name. Assumed in the phrase "May Your name be sanctified" lies both a request for God to act in a manner that sanctifies His name on the earth and an appeal that I would live my life today in a way that would sanctify God's name through everything I do and say. It's a prayer that finds its fulfillment in Jesus' statement, "Let your light so shine before me that they may see your good works and give glory to your Father who is in heaven" (Matt. 5:16). His name is at stake in us.

SCRIPTURE READINGS:

- Read Matthew 6:9–13; Numbers 20:1–13; and Amos 2:6–7.
- In Numbers 20:1–13, how did Moses disobey God?
- How has God "sanctified" His name in the world?
- How do we "sanctify the name of the Lord"?

PRAYER

Father in heaven, may Your name be sanctified.

May my words and my actions make Your name known.

I trust in You and will obey Your word.

Let Your greatness be seen through me.

OUR GOD REIGNS

"May Your kingdom come . . ."

MATTHEW 6:10

The kingship of God, as an idea, appears throughout the Bible. God, as Creator, stands as king over His creation, but because of humanity's rebellion against God, His kingship is realized wherever He makes Himself known or His subjects obey His commands. The phrase "kingdom of heaven" occurs on the lips of Jesus more than any other phrase in the Gospels, yet it is one of the most misunderstood phrases by Christians.

The key to understanding it starts with the language of the phrase. In the first century, Jews who sought to honor the name of God by not pronouncing it used "heaven" as one of several words to refer to God. So, the mention of "heaven" doesn't refer to the dwelling place of God but to God Himself. In English, "kingdom" denotes a physical place, but in Hebrew, the language of Jesus, "kingdom" is a verbal noun (*malkhut*) and would be better translated as "reign" or "authority." The phrase "kingdom of heaven," then, means "the reign (authority) of God."

In the Lord's Prayer, the phrase "May Your kingdom come" could suggest a future realization of the "coming" of God's reign, but the actual sense of the language suggests the idea of "making one king" or "establishing one as king." It would be better, then, to read the phrase in the Lord's Prayer as "May You continue establishing Your reign." An ancient Jewish prayer parallels this sentiment in the Lord's Prayer: "May He establish His kingdom (reign) in the world which He created according to His will."

Outside of the Gospels, the phrase "kingdom of heaven" only appears in rabbinic literature. For the Jewish sages, the "kingdom of heaven" anticipated a future time when God's rule would be revealed to all the inhabitants of the world. In Bible times, Israel toiled under the yoke of foreign rule, but in the future, when God's reign would be revealed, foreign domination would be broken. The sages explained that Israel's subjugation to foreign dominion stemmed from the peoples' disobedience to God's commands. If the people would repent and submit to the rule of God, He would remove the burden of foreign rule. Their repentance could hasten the realization of God's rule.

This sentiment is captured in the statement: "As long as Israel does the will of God, no nation or kingdom shall rule over it. But, if they do not do His will, He will deliver them into the hand of the lowest nation and not only this, but under the legs of the beast of the lowest nation."[6] In this way, the "kingdom of heaven" didn't refer solely to the future; people could presently live in the "kingdom of heaven" by submitting to God's rule and reign and acknowledging His right to rule by obeying His commands. It was the daily recognition and submission to God's rule that led the Jewish sages of Jesus' day to identify the reciting of the Shema, "Hear O Israel, the LORD our God, the LORD is One" (Deut. 6:4), as one's acceptance of the kingdom of heaven.

Obedience to God's commands establishes His rule presently, while in the future it will be revealed to the entire world. Moreover, if the people of God seek to obey Him daily, His rule will be realized upon the earth: "If Israel kept the words of the law given to them, no people or kingdom would rule over them. And what does the law say? 'Take upon you the yoke of My kingdom and emulate one another in the fear of God and practice kindness to one another.'" The injunction to "emulate one another in the fear of God and practice of kindness to one another" parallels Jesus' command to "love God" and "your neighbor who is like yourself." For Jesus and the sages of Israel, a large component of God's rule being realized on earth pertained to the way people treated each other. Obedience to God's commands is not an abstract idea but is actualized through care and concern for others.

The request of the Lord's Prayer for God to continue establishing His reign parallels the request for His name to be sanctified, for His reign is established and His name is sanctified when His people obey His will. He is the King, and our job is to bring ourselves daily into submission to His will and commands. In doing so, we cause His reign to be realized upon the earth.

SCRIPTURE READINGS:

- Read Matthew 6:9–13 and Deuteronomy 6.
- Why is it difficult to submit to God's rule?
- In what ways do you see God's rule and reign in the world today?
- In the past week, what has been the moment when you would say you were furthest from obeying God's rule and reign?
- In the past week, what has been the moment when you were closest to obeying God's rule and reign?

PRAYER

O Lord, our Heavenly Father, continue to establish Your reign.

According to Your will, have Your way in me.

Forgive me for my disobedience.

Deliver me from my sins and help me obey Your word.

DOING GOD'S WILL

May Your will be done on earth as it is in heaven.

MATTHEW 6:10

Jewish prayers frequently request that God act on earth as He does in heaven: "Do Your will in heaven and grant satisfaction to those who fear You on earth. Do what is good in Your eyes. Blessed is He who hears prayer," or "We sanctify Your name in this world as it is sanctified in the highest heavens." This almost goes without saying because the very act of praying seeks to connect us with God and form a bridge between the world we live in and His divine abode.

In the first century, like today, the "will of God" was a distinguishing theological concept. In Jesus' day, questions about how God's will was accomplished were divided by the three main groups within Judaism. For the Pharisees, doing the will of God equaled obeying His commands: "I delight to do Your will, O my God; Your law is within my heart" (Ps. 40:8). One sage stated, "Do His will as if it were your will that He may do your will as if it were His will. Nullify your will before His will that He may nullify the will of others before your will." The Pharisees believed that certain events were the prerogative of God's will, but not all events. Matters of righteous and wicked behavior remained within human choice. On the other hand, the Essenes, the group responsible for the Dead Sea Scrolls, believed that God predetermined everything and nothing happened apart from His will, including the actions of the righteous and the wicked. This belief in absolute predeterminism led them to isolate themselves from the world, particularly the wicked, who didn't belong to their group.

Jesus' outlook in the Lord's Prayer follows the view of the Pharisees with regard to the will of God. In part, God's will is performed whenever His people obey Him; thus, the essence of the prayer requests that we may do His will perfectly here on earth as it is done in heaven. In this way, the request for His will to be done parallels the requests for His kingdom (reign) to be established and His name to be sanctified. All three actions seek the same thing and will be achieved through obedience to His commandments (will).

The Jewish sages frequently connected Israel's hopes for redemption to obedience to God's commands (His will): "Sovereign of the universe, it is well known to You that our will is to do Your will. [But] what prevents us? The yeast in the dough [i.e., our own evil desires] and [our] enslavement to other kingdoms. May it be Your will to save us from them so that we can once more fully perform the statutes of Your will."[7] Jesus, likewise, associated our obedience to God's will with entry into the kingdom of heaven and the redemptive hopes of Israel (Luke 4:16–30; Matt. 4:17; Isa. 58:6–9; 61:1–2). Jesus also saw that obstacles hindered our ability to fully obey God (Matt. 6:13; Luke 8:5–8), yet our earnest desire must be to do His will daily. In some measure, part of the secret to accomplishing this lies in our willingness to submit to His reign and live lives that sanctify His name wherever we find ourselves.

Unlike the Essenes, Jesus believed that our obedience affects God's will being done on earth. He didn't accept a worldview that embraced predeterminism, but rather called upon people to choose daily to submit to God's will and to seek to do it on earth perfectly, as it is done in heaven. Jesus, like his Jewish contemporaries, viewed such obedient submission as preparatory for redemption.

SCRIPTURE READINGS:

- Read Matthew 6:9–13 and Psalm 40.
- How do you know what God's will is for you?
- When there is no clear scriptural direction, how do you make a decision about obeying God's will?
- Why is it important to know and to do God's will?

PRAYER

Father in heaven, may Your name be sanctified in me.

Let Your rule and reign be seen by my obedience to Your will.

Help me to know Your will.

Give me the wisdom, desire, and strength to see it done

THE NEEDS OF TODAY

"Give us this day our daily bread."

MATTHEW 6:11

The phrase "Give us this day our daily bread" reflects Jesus' radical conviction that each day contains its own blessing (Matt. 6:24–34; Luke 12:22–31). He concluded that to seek one's provision beyond the day expressed anxiety and worry, which, for Jesus, marked a person as being "of little faith" and like the pagan Gentiles (Matt. 6:30–32). The unusual Hebrew phrase behind "our daily bread" literally means "the bread that is needful for us." In other words, what we need for sustenance today.

This phrase appears only once in the Old Testament in the words of Agur recorded in the book of Proverbs: "Remove far from me falsehood and lying; give me neither poverty nor riches; feed me with the food that I need (literally, my daily bread)" (30:8). The fuller context of the prayer of Agur certainly has meaning for the thrust of the Lord's Prayer: ". . . or I shall be full and deny you, and say, 'Who is the LORD?' or I shall be poor, and steal, and profane the name of my God" (v. 9). In this request, Agur recognized his dependence upon God and his confident trust in God as the daily source of provision.

Jesus' radical conclusion that we should focus upon the need of the moment only belonged to a stream of Jewish thought that viewed each day as possessing its own sanctity, which requires us to praise God for the present day alone (Matt. 6:34). "It was told of Shammai the Elder: Whenever he found a fine portion he said, 'This will be for the Sabbath.' If later he found a finer one, he put aside the second for the Sabbath. But Hillel the Elder had a different way, for all his works were for the sake of Heaven; he used to say, 'Blessed be the Lord day by day' (Ps. 68:19)." Hillel's emphasis on the sanctity of the present day expressed a firm belief and unrelenting trust in God for today. He also used to say, "'Bad news shall have no terror for him (i.e., the righteous man), because his heart is steadfast, trusting the LORD' (Ps. 112:7). He who trusts in the Lord, bad news shall have no terror for him." Whether or not the bad news is true, according to Hillel, the person who trusts in God becomes immune to bad news because such a person cannot be "anxious about tomorrow" (Matt. 6:34).

The origin of this worldview derived from the miracle of manna ("daily bread") in the wilderness where the Israelites could only "gather enough for that day" (Exod. 16:4–10). The people had to rely on God daily for the provision of the day (Ex. 16:4; Deut. 8:2–4; Luke 4:4). Jewish sages of Jesus' day commented on the biblical phrase "a day's portion every day" (Ex. 16:4): "This means that a man may not gather on one day the portion for the next day. . . . He who created the day has also created its sustenance. . . . He who has enough food to eat for today and says, 'What will I eat tomorrow?' Behold he is of little faith."

Jesus, like His contemporaries, viewed worry and anxiety as a hallmark of those of "little faith." In fact, He went so far as to compare those who worry about food, drink, clothing, and shelter with pagans, who don't acknowledge the God of Israel (Matt. 6:25–34;

Luke 12:22–31). Jesus' words in Matthew 6:25–34 echo a statement made by a Jewish contemporary: "In all the days of your life
have you ever seen a wild animal or a bird laboring in a vocation?
Yet, they are provided for without anxiety. They were created to
serve me, but I was created to serve my Maker. How much more
then should I be provided for without anxiety."[8]

Jesus concluded His statement about worry and anxiety by stating,
"Instead, seek His kingdom (rule), and these things shall be yours
as well" (Luke 12:31). If I seek daily to accept God's rule and submit myself to it, His responsibility is to take care of the things that
I need. In this, Jesus reflects an idea we find among the Jewish
sages: "Whoever receives upon himself the yoke of the Torah (i.e.,
the kingdom of heaven/God's commandments), from him the yoke
of the kingdom (i.e., foreign rule) and the yoke of worldly care will
be removed; but whoever casts off the yoke of the Torah, upon him
will be laid the yoke of the kingdom and the yoke of worldly care."[9]

We can acknowledge God's rule and submit through obedience,
or we can give way to worry and anxiety, which Jesus identified as
paganism because it fails to acknowledge the King of the universe.
The request "Give us this day our daily bread" reminded Jesus'
disciples of God, who provided manna for the children of Israel in
the wilderness, of God the source of all provision and needs of life.
It reminded them that because He is Father we don't have to worry
or be anxious because He takes care of us. We live in a world consumed with anxiety and worry. Does our visible, daily trust in the
living God demonstrate our confidence in our Father in heaven, or
is our "paganism" prohibiting those around us from coming near to
Him, the source of all provision?

SCRIPTURE READINGS:

- Read Matthew 6:9–13, 25–34; Luke 12:22–31; and Proverbs 30:1–9.
- What are you worrying about today?
- What are some of your greatest worries and concerns?
- How can you demonstrate confidence that your heavenly Father will provide for you?

PRAYER

Lord, my heavenly Father, help me to trust in You.

I acknowledge Your rule and reign in my life.

Help me obey You and keep me from anxiety and worry.

Provide for my needs today.

YOUR NEIGHBOR WHO IS LIKE YOURSELF

———

"Forgive us . . . as we have forgiven."

MATTHEW 6:12

n the centuries prior to the first century AD, Judaism underwent a theological revolution that emphasized a new sensitivity: People were to serve God with unconditional love, without any thought of reward. This new religious sensitivity crystalized around two biblical passages: "You shall love the LORD your God" (Deut. 6:5) and "you shall love your neighbor" (Lev. 19:18; Luke 10:27). Equally important in this developing sensitivity was the verse from Genesis 1:27: "And God created man in His image." Every human being bears the image of God; therefore, each person has immediate value and possibility. The saying of Rabbi Shimeon ben Elazar makes this connection explicit: "This word 'Love your neighbor as yourself' has been proclaimed with a 'great oath': I—the Lord, have created him (i.e., your neighbor). If you love him, I can be relied upon to reward you, but if you do not love him—I can be relied upon to visit my judgment upon you."[10]

This realization led Judaism to read Leviticus 19:18 as "Love your neighbor who is like yourself." Writing in the second century BC, Jesus ben Sira stated, "Forgive your neighbor the wrong he has done, and then your sins will be pardoned when you pray. Does anyone harbor anger against another and expect healing from the Lord? If one has no mercy toward another like himself, can he then seek pardon for his own sins? If a mere mortal harbors wrath, who will make an atoning sacrifice for his sins? . . . Remember the commandments, and do not be angry with your neighbor, remember the covenant of the Most High, and overlook faults."[11] In the circles that embraced this new sensitivity, love of one's neighbor became a precondition for reconciliation with God. Or to put it a little differently, "God will act towards me in the manner I act towards others because I am more like them than I am like God." Another sage stated, "The word 'Love your neighbor as yourself' was proclaimed on Mount Sinai with an oath: 'If you hate your neighbor whose deeds are wicked like your own, I, the Lord, will punish you as your judge; but if you love your neighbor whose deeds are good like your own, I, the Lord, will be faithful to you and have mercy on you'"[12] (Matt. 25:34–46).

Jesus embraced this new sensitivity and expected His disciples to do the same: "Blessed are the merciful (i.e., those who show mercy), for they will receive mercy" (Matt. 5:7). Jesus felt that the status of my relationship with God is found in my relationship with others; in fact, if I have broken relationships, it falls to me to reconcile with my neighbor before I seek reconciliation with God: "So if you are offering your gift at the altar, and there remember that your brother has something against you, leave your gift there before the altar (which was in Jerusalem) and go; first be reconciled to your brother, and then come and offer your gift" (vv. 23–24). Jesus' words are similar to a sage who lived shortly after him: "Transgressions between a man and his neighbor are not expiated by the Day of Atonement unless the man first makes peace with his neighbor."

In the Lord's Prayer, Jesus enjoined His disciples to pray, "Forgive us . . . as we have forgiven" (Matt. 6:12). In other words, He felt our forgiveness from God was proportional to the forgiveness we have shown to others. He concluded the Lord's Prayer with the statement: "For if you forgive men their trespasses, your Father also will forgive you; but if you do not forgive men their trespasses, neither will your Father forgive your trespasses" (vv. 14–15). Once we become sensitized to this revolutionary thought within Judaism, we see how deeply it impacted Jesus' message. It appears everywhere—in His sayings and parables and in His actions. Based upon this new sensitivity, Jesus drew the radical conclusion that we should love our enemies, those who hate us (Matt. 5:43–48; Luke 6:27–36), "There must be no limit in your goodness, as your heavenly Father's goodness knows no bounds" (Matt. 5:48). In this way, Jesus called on His disciples to imitate God through their mercy and forgiveness to others, realizing they are like us.

Jesus' message of mercy and compassion towards others has profound possibilities in our world to offer healing and reconciliation. Whether within families, communities, or between races and countries, this message can transform our world and change lives, and through our mercy, bring God's mercy into difficult situations. So today, let us pray, "Forgive us . . . as we have forgiven."

SCRIPTURE READINGS:

- Read Matthew 6:9–15; Leviticus 19:9–18; Matthew 25:31–46; and Luke 6:27–36.
- Why is forgiveness such an important element of love?
- What makes forgiveness so difficult to do?
- Is there someone you need to show love to or forgive?

PRAYER

Father God, thank You for Your forgiveness.

May I show Your love by forgiving those who have hurt me.

Let there be no limit to the goodness that I give to others.

Forgive me as I have forgiven others.

FEARING SIN

"And do not bring us into the grasp of temptation,
but deliver us from evil."

MATTHEW 6:13

J ewish prayers, like Jewish poetry, made frequent use of parallelism, which is where one statement reinforces another. The phrases "And do not bring us into the grasp of temptation, but deliver us from evil" in the Lord's Prayer stand parallel to each other; the one reinforces the other.

The request for God's deliverance from temptation and evil appears frequently in Jewish prayers (Ps. 119:113). For example one prayer entreated God, "May it be Your will . . . to make us familiar with Your Torah and to make us adhere to Your commandments, and do not bring us into the grasp of sin, transgression, and iniquity, nor the grasp of temptation and disgrace. Let the evil inclination not rule over us. Keep us away from a bad man and a bad companion."[13] The request for God's assistance and deliverance from temptation grows from the realization of sin's insidious, destructive nature and our need for God's assistance. More importantly, it places the supplicant in a position of submission to God, relying upon His help.

Jesus belonged to a stream of Jewish piety that was characterized by its fear of sin. A Jewish contemporary of Jesus stated, "Anyone whose fear of sin precedes his wisdom, his wisdom endures; but anyone whose wisdom precedes his fear of sin, his wisdom does not endure."[14] We see this in Jesus' statement, "Whoever then relaxes one of the least of these commandments and teaches men so, shall be called least in the kingdom of heaven; but he who does them and teaches them shall be called great in the kingdom of heaven" (Matt. 5:19). Jesus and His contemporaries saw sin as corruptive and destructive, not only to an individual but to a community. For this reason, they urged people to flee even the appearance of sin: "Keep aloof from that which leads to sin and whatever resembles sin. Shudder from committing a minor transgression, lest you be led to commit a major transgression; hasten to perform a minor precept, for, thereby you will be led to perform a major precept"[15] (Matt. 23:23). In other words, if you endeavor to obey God in the smallest of matters, you will obey Him in the big ones; if you allow a little disobedience to exist in your life, soon you will disobey in big matters.

This attitude stands behind Jesus' discussion concerning murder, adultery, swearing falsely, and retaliation in Matthew 5 (vv. 21–30, 33–42). In each of these instances, Jesus' instructions emphasize the governing principle: If you keep away from things that lead to sin, even a minor transgression, you will never violate the commandments of God. For example, if you control your anger towards another person, you will never murder; if you don't allow yourself to lust after another, you will never commit adultery.

A teaching that circulated at the time of Jesus was called the "Two Ways." It referred to the "way of life" and the "way of death."[16] The "Two Ways" influenced Jesus as can be seen from this statement of its caution to fear even the appearance of sin:

"My son, flee from all evil and from everything which resembles it. Be not angry, for anger leads to murder. My son, do not be lustful, for lust leads to adultery. My son, regard not omens, for this leads to idolatry. My son, be not a liar, for lying leads to theft. My son, be not a grumbler, for this leads to blasphemy" (Didache 3:1–6; Matt. 5:21–30, 33–42).

The fear of sin caused Jesus and His contemporaries to recognize that the path of sin ("the way of death") is subtle: "The beginning of transgression is impure thought, the second stage is scoffing, the third stage is haughtiness, the fourth stage is roughness, the fifth stage is idleness, the sixth stage is causeless hatred and the seventh stage an evil (non-generous) eye."[17] The ease with which sin entangles led them to say, "Keep aloof from everything hideous and from whatever seems hideous, lest others suspect you of transgression."[18]

For Jesus, sin was an act of disobedience committed against the commandments of God. He viewed it as destructive, corruptive, and insidious, both to the community and the individual. This is why He repeatedly cautioned His followers about even the appearance of evil and seeking to perform "the least of these commandments." His fear of sin led Him to instruct His disciples to pray: "And do not bring us into the grasp of temptation, but deliver us from evil." We live in a world that has lost its fear of sin. As followers of Jesus, we would do well to remember that those who do the least of these commandments and teach others to do so will be called "great in the kingdom of heaven."

SCRIPTURE READINGS:

- Read Matthew 6:9–13 and 5:17–48.
- What is the difference between a "fear of sin" and legalism?
- What are "the least of these commandments"?
- "The way of death" begins with impure thoughts. How do you curb impure thoughts?

PRAYER

Our Father in heaven, let Your name be sanctified in me.

Rule and reign in my life and in the world.

May Your will be done on earth as it is in heaven.

Provide for my daily needs and calm my anxiousness.

Forgive me as I forgive others.

Keep me from the grasp of temptation.

GOD IS FOR US

"Glory to God in the highest, on earth peace,
goodwill to all mankind."

LUKE 2:14

I f you grew up reading the King James Bible or watching *A Charlie Brown Christmas*, you're probably familiar with the three-part hymn of the angels announcing the birth of Jesus to the shepherds: 1) Glory to God in the highest, 2) on earth peace, and 3) goodwill to all mankind. Most modern translations reflect a two-part hymn: 1) Glory to God in the highest, 2) on earth peace among men with whom He is pleased.

The difference between these two readings derives from a variant spelling of a Greek word within the manuscripts of Luke's Gospel. The threefold angelic proclamation comes from manuscripts containing the Greek word εὐδοκία, "goodwill," in the nominative case: "on earth peace, goodwill toward men." The twofold proclamation comes from the reading εὐδοκίας. The addition of the letter sigma (ς: pronounced like the English letter "s") at the end of the word puts it in the genitive case: "and on earth, peace among men of his will." The difference of one letter significantly changes the meaning of the angelic proclamation from God's goodwill being directed toward all mankind, to His peace resting solely upon those of His will, i.e., the elect. Both readings reflect two competitive worldviews within Jewish society in the first century.

The threefold angelic proclamation declares a more universal message of God's goodwill toward all humans (Luke 2:10). Jewish literature of the Greco-Roman period contains numerous angelic songs; all angelic songs found in the literature of this period derive from two angelic utterances in the Old Testament: Isaiah 6:3, "Holy, holy, holy is the LORD of hosts; the whole earth is full of his glory," and Ezekiel 3:12, "Blessed be the glory of the LORD from his place." The threefold "holy" of the angels in Isaiah 6:3 provided a literary structure for angelic prayers within later Jewish literature. The Aramaic translation (targum) of Isaiah 6:3 interpreted the song of the angels: "Holy—in the highest heaven, the house of his presence, Holy—upon the earth, the work of his might, Holy—for endless ages is the LORD of hosts; the whole earth is full of the brightness of his glory." This expansion of the angelic message in Isaiah 6:3 is strikingly similar to the threefold blessing of the angels found in Luke 2:14: "Glory to God in the highest [Holy—in the highest heaven, the house of his presence], on earth peace [Holy—upon the earth, the work of his might], goodwill toward men [Holy—for endless ages is the Lord of hosts]."

The angels told the shepherds that their message of good news "will come to all people" (Luke 2:10). God's goodwill is not simply for the elect; it extends to everyone, for "He makes His sun rise on the evil and on the good, and sends rain on the just and the unjust" (Matt. 5:45). His merciful will reaches out to all people to bring peace, completeness, and wholeness. And, in the birth of Jesus, God has drawn near to demonstrate within the bounds of history what His will is, to give voice and example to His will (Heb. 1:1–2).

The message of the angels was an announcement of God's nearness. In the incarnation of Jesus, God entered into time and space. God is for us, and He has drawn near to us. God is a part of human history; therefore, there is hope. God hasn't turned a blind eye to the suffering of the righteous or a deaf ear to the cry of the afflicted. His mercy extends to all people, and He will redeem us. To understand the incarnation is to enter into the world of Jesus, when God entered a specific time at a specific space in history (Gal. 4:4). In this act, God revealed Himself to us, so in this world filled with fear, uncertainty, and turmoil, we should take a moment to meditate and declare with the angels, "Glory to God in the highest, on earth peace, goodwill toward men."

SCRIPTURE READINGS:

- Read Luke 2:1–20 and Hebrews 1.
- Why do you think God chose that particular time and place for Jesus to come to earth?
- What is the significance of the incarnation?
- When and where do you feel God's nearness?

PRAYER

Glory to God, I invite You to come near.

May Your name be exalted in heaven and on earth.

Allow Your peace to announce Your rule and reign.

Let Your goodwill be done in our world.

Maxim nopolis

Megiddo

N   A

M

Samaria

H.
Gerixim M.

K

Temp. Samaritan

Bet

B   E   N

Nicopo.
v. Emma

HIEROSO

Bethlehem

ENDNOTES

---

1. *Hermenia*, trans. Linda M. Maloney (Minneapolis: Fortress Press, 2011),

2. Incidentally the geographic description of the mountains surrounding Jerusalem helps to date the psalm. During the reign of Hezekiah, Jerusalem expanded to include the western hill (modern-day Mount Zion), which was higher. The topographical description of the psalm means that it was written when Jerusalem occupied the eastern hill only, i.e., prior to the reign of Hezekiah.

3. Percy Bysshe Shelley, *Shelley: Poems* (New York: Everyman's Library Publishing, 1993), 81.

4. Deuteronomy Rabbah 2.24.

5. Mekhilta de Rabbi Ishmael to Exodus 15:2.

6. Mekhilta de Rabbi Ishmael to Exodus 19:1; Sifre Deuteronomy, 305; Avot de Rabbi Nathan version A, 17.

7. B. Berachot 17a.

8. M. Kiddushin 4.14.

9. M. Avot 3.5.

10. Avot de Rabbi Nathan version A, 16.

11. Ben Sira 28:2–5, 7.

12. Avot de Rabbi Nathan version A, 26.

13. Prayer recited before the morning service.

14. M. Avot 3.9.

15. Derekh Eretz Zuta 2.16–17.

16. See Didache 1:1.

17. Derekh Eretz Zuta 4.10.

18. Derekh Eretz Zuta 1.13.

PHOTO CREDITS

---

1. All photographs courtesy of thinkstock.com

2. Photos on pages 84, 102, 128, and 132 belong to The Center for Holy Land Studies and are used by permission.

ABOUT THE AUTHOR

—

Marc Turnage was born in Springfield, Missouri. After graduating from Evangel University with a BA in Biblical Studies, he moved to Jerusalem, Israel, where he studied at Jerusalem University College and earned an MA in Jewish History and New Testament Backgrounds. During his time in Israel, Marc studied with professors R. Steven Notley, David Flusser, Michael Stone, Hanan and Esther Eshel, Chana Safrai, Michael Sokoloff, and Gabriel Barkay. After completing his MA, Marc began his post-graduate studies at Bar Ilan University in Ramat Gan, Israel, under the supervision of the late Professor Hanan Eshel. He is currently finishing his PhD at Bar Ilan under the supervision of Professor Esther Eshel.

During his tenure in Israel and afterward, Marc guided study tours of university students and professors and cross-denominational Christian groups from around the world. He and his family relocated to Springfield, Missouri, where he served on the faculties of Missouri State University, Evangel University, Drury University, and the Assemblies of God Theological Seminary.

In December 2009, Marc was appointed by the executive presbytery of the General Council of the Assemblies of God as the director of the Center for Holy Lands Studies (CHLS), a historic endeavor to educate Assemblies of God constituents in the physical, historical, and cultural settings of the Bible.

Subscribe to Marc's blog and follow him on Facebook and Twitter:

- Blog: The Shard and the Scroll (theshardandthescroll.com)
- Facebook: Marc Turnage
- Twitter: @MarcTurnage

Maximianopolis

Megiddo

Fl.

M A N A

X M

Samaria

H. Gerizim M.
Temp. Samaritan

Bet

B E N

Nicopo
v. Emma

HIEROSO

Bethlehem

FOR MORE INFORMATION

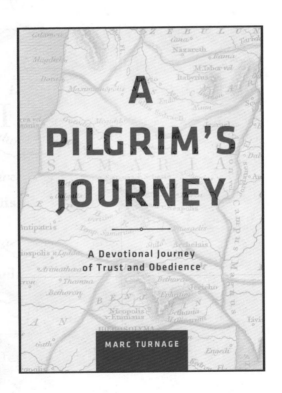

For more information about this and other valuable resources
visit www.myhealthychurch.com.